For This Is Right

A practical application of
The Fifth Commandment
for young people

Based on Scripture
and the
**Westminster
Larger Catechism**

Compiled by Pam Forster

Doorposts
5905 SW Lookingglass Drive, Gaston, OR 97119

ISBN 13: 978-1-891206-22-1
ISBN 10: 1-891206-22-2

Catechism questions are taken from:
The Westminster Larger Catechism
Published by Great Commission Publications
3640 Windsor Park Drive, Suite 100
Suwanee, GA 30024-1800

Definitions are taken from:
Noah Webster's 1828 American Dictionary of the English Language
Published by The Foundation for American Christian Education
P.O. Box 27035
San Francisco, CA 94127

Unless otherwise noted, all Scripture verses are quoted from
The King James Version

Scripture quotations marked "NKJV"
are taken from the **New King James Version®**.
Copyright © 1982 by Thomas Nelson, Inc.
Used by permission. All rights reserved.

Scripture quotations marked "NASB" are taken from
the **New American Standard Bible®**.

Copyright © 1960, 1962, 1963, 1968, 1971, 1972, 1973,
1975, 1977, 1995 by The Lockman Foundation
Used by permission. (www.Lockman.org)

Doorposts
5905 SW Lookingglass Drive, Gaston, OR 97119

Thank You

This book has been written during a challenging time in our family's life. Thank you to those of you who ministered God's grace to us in special ways. We have been greatly blessed as the recipients; may you be even more blessed as the givers.

Thank you to our Bethany Rose who took great delight in planning, preparing, presenting, and cleaning up beautiful and delicious meals for Daniel and me as we spent some concentrated time away from home in front of our computers. Your humor certainly livened up our days!

Thank you to Johanna who kept the rest of the family fed and laundered while we were away!

Thanks to Susannah who beautified my desk with flowers and treats and pretty cups of tea, and didn't cry when I dumped my just-delivered glass of ice water into the laundry basket full of books and papers we had just shoveled off the desk.

Daniel, you continue to amaze me with your patience and skill. You (and God) are responsible for any sanity that I still possess at the end of a book project.

You are all great blessings to me! It is a joy to watch you mature into godly, cheerful servants of Christ!

This book is dedicated to my father,

Calvin Donald Mohr

Thank you, Daddy, for your constant love
and your faithful prayers.

Thank you for the example
and encouragement
your life has been to me and my children.

You have shown us
how to work and how to rest,
how to give and how to receive,
how to be tough and how to be tender.

It is a delight
to honor you as my father.

Forward

Our society challenges authority at every turn. Why should a wife submit her will to that of her husband? Why should a child obey his parents? Why show respect to a teacher or police officer? Why give a boss a full, honest day's work? Why, in our day when most everyone does what is right in his own eyes, should anyone be expected to put himself under the authority of another?

God tells us that He exercises His sovereign authority over us through His ordained representatives. Romans 13:1 states, "Let every soul be subject unto the higher powers. For there is no power but of God: the powers that be are ordained of God."

He has ordained relationships of authority for our benefit and for the benefit of those around us. Paul, in Romans 13, goes on to say, "For rulers are not a terror to good works, but to the evil. Wilt thou then not be afraid of the power? do that which is good, and thou shalt have praise of the same: for he is the minister of God to thee for good. But if thou do that which is evil, be afraid; for he beareth not the sword in vain: for he is the minister of God, a revenger to execute wrath upon him that doeth evil."

It is my prayer that this book will put the powerful truth of God's timeless Word into the hands of you, children and young people, to instruct and strengthen you in your God-given role. Obey God by obeying your parents, and they will be "ministers of God" to you for good.

It is my prayer that these same words of Scripture, powerful, timeless, and true, will also be an encouragement to you parents as you minister to your children by leading and discipling them. You are, by God's appointment, His ministers.

The Westminster Larger Catechism and This Study

In the mid-1600's, at the request of the English Parliament, the Westminster Assembly of Divines gathered at Westminster Abbey. They were asked to write a confession that would help establish uniform worship and church polity throughout the kingdoms of England, Scotland, and Ireland. The result, in 1648, was the **Westminster Confession of Faith**, a document that would become foundational to the theology of English-speaking Congregational, Reformed, and Presbyterian churches. It is a creed that faithfully and concisely preserves and clarifies fifteen centuries of Christian thought and teaching from the Scriptures.

The **Westminster Larger and Shorter Catechisms**, which are basically abridgements of the **Confession of Faith**, are valuable teaching tools that have been used throughout the centuries by protestant pastors, teachers, and parents. This book is based on Questions 123-128 of the **Westminster Larger Catechism**. These questions study and detail the meaning of the Fifth Commandment. How do we honor our fathers and mothers? In what ways do we demonstrate a failure to honor them as God has commanded?

Q. 123. Which is the fifth commandment?

A. The fifth commandment is, **Honor thy father and mother; that thy days may be long upon the land which the Lord thy God giveth thee.**

Q. 124. Who are meant by **father** and **mother** in the fifth commandment?

A. By **father** and **mother**, in the fifth commandment, are meant, not only natural parents, but all superiors in age and gifts; and especially such as, by God's ordinance, are over us in place of authority, whether in family, church, or commonwealth.

Q. 125. Why are superiors styled **Father** and **Mother**?

A. Superiors are styled **Father** and **Mother**, both to teach them in all duties toward their inferiors, like natural parents, to express love and tenderness to them, according to their several relations; and to work inferiors to a greater willingness and cheerfulness in performing their duties to their superiors, as to their parents.

Q. 126. What is the general scope of the fifth commandment?

A. The general scope of the fifth commandment is, the performance of those duties which we mutually owe in our several relations, as inferiors, superiors, or equals.

Q. 127. What is the honor that inferiors owe to their superiors?

A. The honor which inferiors owe to their superiors is, all due reverence in heart, word, and behavior; prayer and thanksgiving for them; imitation of their virtues and graces; willing obedience to their lawful commands and counsels; due submission to their corrections; fidelity to, defense and maintenance of their persons and authority, according to their several ranks, and the nature *of their places; bearing with their infirmities, and covering them in love, that so they may be an honor to them and to their government.*

Q. 128. What are the sins of inferiors against their superiors?

A. The sins of inferiors against their superiors are, all neglect of the duties required toward them; envying at, contempt of, and rebellion against, their persons and places, in their lawful counsels, commands, and corrections; cursing, mocking, and all such refractory and scandalous carriage, as proves a shame and dishonor to them and their government.

For the purposes of this book, we have focused on the child's relationship with his parents. However, the catechism helps us understand that the principles of the Fifth Commandment apply to any superior-inferior relationship. The terms "superior" and "inferior" are terms of rank or position. They do not imply that one person is better than another; they are simply describing the two roles of authority and follower. The term "superior" refers to one who is in a position of authority over another. In the same way, "inferior" refers to the person who is under that authority.

This book is designed to help sons and daughters better understand their relationship and duties to their parents. However, many of the questions and Scriptures presented in this book will also apply, at least in principle and often in detail, to relationships with teachers, law enforcement agents, governmental representatives, employers, grandparents, and other authorities.

Table of Contents and Daily Checklist

Use this set of questions as a daily evaluation and as a table of contents for the rest of the book. Read and answer these questions at the end of each day. Your honest answers will help uncover problem areas. The page numbers listed with each question will direct you to further study and questions related to each evaluation question.

The Whole Duty of Man

"Let us hear the conclusion of the whole matter: fear God, and keep his commandments: for this is the whole duty of man." (Ecclesiastes 12:13)

God's directions for us are not complex – **fear Him, and do what He says**. Sounds simple, doesn't it? But as we all know, these directions are not so easy to obey.

- **Dead in our sins,** we are incapable of even understanding God's commands until He, in His great mercy, empowers us. Through the saving work of Jesus on the cross, He draws us to Himself and makes us alive in Him. *"But God, who is rich in mercy, for his great love wherewith he loved us, even when we were dead in sins, hath quickened us together with Christ, (by grace ye are saved)." (Ephesians 2:4-5)*

- Saved from bondage to sin and death, we are **new creatures**. *"Therefore if any man be in Christ, he is a new creature: old things are passed away; behold, all things are become new." (2 Corinthians 5:17)*

- We are **no longer sin's slaves.** *"Therefore, brethren, we are debtors, not to the flesh, to live after the flesh." (Romans 8:12)*

- We are **freed to serve and obey our Lord**. *"Being then made free from sin, ye became the servants of righteousness" (Romans 6:18). "For we are his workmanship, created in Christ Jesus unto good works, which God hath before ordained that we should walk in them." (Ephesians 2:10)*

- However, although we desire to serve God, **we still do battle against our flesh**, and will until our earthly lives end. *"For the flesh lusteth against the Spirit, and the Spirit against the flesh: and these are contrary the one to the other: so that ye cannot do the things that ye would." (Galatians 5:17)*

- We are called to **give ourselves to God**. *"I beseech you therefore, brethren, by the mercies of God, that ye present your bodies a living sacrifice, holy, acceptable unto God, which is your reasonable service. And be not conformed to this world: but be ye transformed by the renewing of your mind, that ye may prove what is that good, and acceptable, and perfect, will of God." (Romans 12:1-2)*

- **God has armed us for the battle against sin and Satan**. *" Finally, my brethren, be strong in the Lord, and in the power of his might. Put on the whole armour of God, that ye may be able to stand against the wiles of the devil. . . Wherefore take unto you the whole armour of God, that ye may be able to withstand in the evil day, and having done all, to stand." (Ephesians 6:10,11, and 13)*

- **Our weapon is God's Word** . *"And take the helmet of salvation, and the sword of the Spirit, which is the word of God." (Ephesians 6:17)*

For This Is Right is written in order **to arm children and parents with God's Word**. God has commanded children to honor and obey their parents. This commandment is not complicated, but it is not an easy command to obey. Children naturally want to indulge their own desires. They do not willingly choose to submit their will to the will of their parents. Instead, the little two-year-old seeks to exert his will over his parents' will. The older child attempts to avoid the task he has been assigned. The teenager is tempted to treat his parents with disrespect. Obedience to God's command does not come naturally; it requires training and discipline.

This study explores the meaning and practical application of the Fifth Commandment, "Honour thy father and thy mother: that thy days may be long upon the land which the LORD thy God giveth thee" (Exodus 20:12). **A true respect of our parents is foundational to fulfilling our duty to fear and obey God.**

- Obedience to parents, because God has commanded us to obey them, is part of **obedience to God.**

- Obedience to parents, while training a child to submit his will to another, also **trains him to submit his will to his Heavenly Father.**

- A proper reverence for authority will **prepare a child for life-long reverence for God.**

- Obedience to parents will bring **God's blessing,** allowing the child to live in the protection, peace, and true freedom that God provides for those who choose to obey.

The Westminster Larger Catechism, written in the 1600's to instruct believers in the basic tenets of the faith, expands on the meaning of each of the Ten Commandments. We have turned to its instruction on the Fifth Commandment as a guide while considering all the practical, day-to-day ways we can obey this command. What does obedience look like? What does disobedience look like? What does God say about obedience and disobedience?

We will focus on God's Word, because it is the weapon that God has given us for victory. "Wherewithal shall a young man cleanse his way? by taking heed thereto according to thy word. With my whole heart have I sought thee: O let me not wander from thy commandments. Thy word have I hid in mine heart, that I might not sin against thee." (Psalm 119:9-11)

This book will explore the different facets of obedience, and will provide Scripture that instructs us in each area. These verses can be studied, meditated on, memorized, and obeyed.

How To Use "For This Is Right"

This book can be used in many different ways. It can be helpful as:

- **A tool to help young people honestly evaluate their relationship to their parents and other authorities.** With the aid of this book, regular self-examination in the light of God's Word, combined with humble repentance, will help children grow in their obedience to both God and their parents.

- **A teaching tool as parents and children study together God's ordained plan for their relationship together.** This could occur in a family Bible time or a parent-child Bible study.

- **A study for parents,** helping them better understand the role their children should accept under their leadership and authority, and the responsibility they have as parents to train their children in obedience.

- **An aid in counseling situations.** This can include a parent instructing a wayward or rebellious child, a parent offering assistance to another parent, or a counselor seeking to offer family counsel.

A. A Tool for Self-Examination

1. Start by reading pages VII-VIII carefully. These questions and answers are directly quoted from **The Westminster Larger Catechism**. This portion of the catechism is dealing with the practical meaning of the Fifth Commandment. It offers much for the growing child's consideration and meditation.

   What does it mean to "honor thy father and mother"? How do we demonstrate this same respect and reverence in our relationships to other "superiors"? What are specific ways in which we are required to show honor to our superiors? In what specific ways do we commonly sin against our superiors?

   (Please note that the terms "superior" and "inferior" do not imply that those under authority are inferior human beings. They merely mean that those under authority are placed in an "inferior" or lower position functionally. **Noah Webster's 1828 American Dictionary of the English Language** defines "superior" as "one who is more advanced in age" and "one who is more advanced in rank or office." In similar fashion "inferior" is defined as "a person who is younger, or of a lower station or rank in society.")

2. By reading through the "Daily Checklist" (pages IX and X), which follows the catechism questions, you can use this book as a tool for regular self-examination. Each short phrase from the catechism passage is listed in boldface type, and is followed by a question that more directly applies the phrase to the daily life of a son or daughter.

3. If you come across a question that you know you cannot answer in a positive way, you can refer to the page number listed with that question. This will lead you to an entire series of detailed questions and Scripture passages that deal with the same topic.

   For example, under the first heading, "All Due Reverence in Heart," the question asks, "Did I submit to God and His plan for me by humbly respecting and submitting to my parents?" If you must honestly answer "no" to that question, you can then turn to page 9, as listed with its corresponding heading, for an enlarged study of that question.

   The twenty questions in this first section are each designed to help you meditate on the concept of "reverence of heart" as it would apply in your relationship to your parents. With each question you will find Scripture passages to read. Meditate on these Scriptures. Consider their contexts. Think about what these verses teach relative to the roles of "inferiors."

   God's Word is a "lamp unto [our] feet, and a light unto [our] path" (Psalm 119:105). "The entrance of [His] words giveth light" (Psalm 119:130). Submit to His Word as He sheds His light in your heart, bringing encouragement and comfort, instruction and guidance, and also conviction of sin. Believe what God says in His Word, and allow it, by God's gracious working, to change your heart and your actions.

4. Use a highlighter to mark verses that are especially meaningful to you. Memorize the ones that would be encouraging or convicting to you in times of temptation. Use study tools to help you gain a better understanding of specific verses. Use your concordance to find other verses that relate to each question. Pray, using these questions and verses to guide you as you earnestly seek God's direction in your life.

B. A Bible Study for Parents with Their Children

Parents, you can use **For This Is Right** to help you teach your children about godly obedience.

- If your children are old enough, this can take place during your daily family worship time.

- You can also read one question and its attendant Bible verses at each meal, taking time to discuss their meanings and the opportunities for practical application during the day.

- A one-on-one Bible study with a parent and child will also offer many opportunities for instruction and growth as you discuss your relationship together.

C. A Bible Study for Parents

For This Is Right can also provide profitable Bible study material for a husband and wife together.

- Study together the standard of obedience that God expects of your children, and discuss how you will work together to train your children according to that standard.

- Pray together for humble obedience to God's Word and for unity and wisdom as you raise your children for God's glory.

- Pray together for your children's humble response to God's Word and your instruction.

D. An Aid for Counselors

For a young person seeking to encourage or confront a friend, for adults who want to counsel wayward young people or discouraged parents, for counselors and pastors who are helping parents and children work through difficulties, **For This Is Right** offers easily-referenced Scripture to read and discuss, and easy-to-use material for counselees to study.

A Few Words to Sons and Daughters

This book is for you, sons and daughters! In it you will explore the many facets of obedience and disobedience, respect and disrespect. As a son or daughter under the direct authority of your parents, humble obedience is one of your primary callings during this era of your life. It is also one of the most important lessons you must learn before adulthood!

Lamentations 3:27 tells us, "It is good for a man that he bear the yoke in his youth." Authority is not a distasteful thing, designed by God to test us. It is His loving gift. He uses the yoke of authority to protect us and to help us become more like Jesus. Jesus was under authority, living His earthly life as a man, choosing to set aside His powers as God to fulfill His Father's will. He said, "Take my yoke upon you, and learn of me; for I am meek and lowly in heart: and ye shall find rest unto your souls. For my yoke is easy, and my burden is light." (Matthew 11:29-30)

Meekness is not weakness; it is harnessed strength, directed strength, strength brought under discipline. Like a strong and spirited horse that is trained and ready to serve his master, the truly meek and humble child is ready to joyfully serve and submit to his parents. His strengths, energy, and gifts, under discipline, become tools of blessing to himself and all those around him. Safe and secure, surrounded by the hedge of authority that God designed for him, quietly accepting the limitations that God has ordained, the child is free to grow and thrive as God intended.

We've all seen the little child throwing a tantrum in the grocery store. That child is blessed with a strong will! He is, however, misusing it! If he gets what he wants, he will not be content. He will only make more demands at the next store. Allowed over the years to indulge his own selfish desires, this child will live a life of frustration and failure.

Brought under the yoke of his parents' authority, that strong child will learn to accept limitations. The child will be content. His strong will, not crushed, but under authority, may one day be a great blessing to others as the child perseveres in a task while others give up, when he continues to trust God while others fall aside.

God gave each of us a great gift when he placed us under authority. Bear the yoke of authority in your youth! Recognize it as the great blessing that it is! Do not resist, but give God thanks for this evidence of His love.

Then walk as Jesus walked. He provided for us the perfect example of obedience. He "took upon him the form of a servant, and was made in the likeness of men: and being found in fashion as a man, he humbled himself, and became obedient unto death, even the death of the cross" (Philippians 2:7b-8). It is unlikely that God will call any of us to humble ourselves to the point of death on a cross, and none of us, in order to obey, will have to set aside our powers as He did. However, if we want to do our living and dying unto His glory, which is our privilege and pleasure to do, we will have to set aside our desire to be our own god. We will have to submit ourselves to the will of those over us. Whether we live in times of freedom or times of terror, God gives us the grace and strength to do this. Pray for a humble and teachable spirit.

Pray for your parents, too. Ask them how you can pray for them. And remember that God will use you as part of His answers to those prayers! Remember, too, that your parents are fallen humans, just like you. They are not perfect, but God knew that when He appointed them to be your parents. He will work through them to accomplish His perfect will in your life. Trust Him.

A Few Words to Fathers and Mothers

This book is written for your children, but it is also written for you. A full-orbed picture of obedience is presented in these pages. Use this picture to help you better understand the godly obedience that you must strive toward with your children. Commit yourself – your time, your energy, your love, your prayers – to this task that God has given you in this season of your life. Obey God by teaching your children true obedience to you and Him.

Our task as parents is to accurately portray the fatherhood of our Heavenly Father:

- Draw near to your children. Know them, listen to them, talk to them. Spend time with them individually and with the family as a whole.

- Love unconditionally, not just when you feel like it.

- Be consistent. Don't allow moods to govern your decisions and discipline, but be guided by Scripture's truth.

- Discipline sin. Show the mercy that God shows, but don't overlook sin.

- Don't shield your children from the consequences of their sin. Allow them, when possible, to experience and learn from the natural outcomes of their disobedience.

- Be an example of what you teach. Don't attempt to discipline your child in areas in which you are unwilling to be disciplined. Grow in godliness and obedience with your children.

- Have plans for your children. Seek God's guidance as you establish goals for each of them. What are their weaknesses? How can you help them grow in these areas? What projects and experiences will challenge them toward greater maturity?

- As husband and wife, be united together as you care for your family.

The parent's job is challenging. Satan wants to discourage us, distract us, and mislead us. Be prepared for the battle. Arm yourself for the task:

- Study God's Word and pray. Seek wisdom from His Word, and pray for yourself, your spouse, and your children daily. Pray with your children.

- Don't allow other interests or tasks to distract you from this very important job that you can only perform during these years of your life. Guard your time and affections.

- Don't take your child's sins personally. Recognize them as the manifestations of the sin nature your child inherited from Adam through you. Expect sin, and be ready to take advantage of each wrongdoing as an opportunity for instruction and training in righteousness.

- Don't give up. God is faithful. He will give you strength, wisdom, perseverance, and encouragement.

- Don't be afraid to lead your children in righteousness. Love them and God enough to faithfully teach and discipline them, wholly trusting trust God with the results.

- Don't wait until your children are "old enough to understand." Train early in habits of obedience, and point your children to God and His Word as your standard.

Parenting the Compliant Child

Some children make the parenting job look easy. They rarely challenge, almost always do what we ask, continually seek to please, and quickly respond to a simple verbal reproof. If you have more than one child, you have probably come to realize that this is not necessarily a reflection on your excellent parenting skills, but simply the temperament of that particular child!

Thank God for this child's tender spirit, but never take it for granted. In the midst of challenges from more self-willed children in the family, this compliant child can sometimes be neglected. He's easy, perhaps quieter than his siblings, makes few demands, and requires very little aggressive discipline. Don't allow this child to coast through childhood! He still needs your attention and training. Go out of your way to develop a deep relationship with him. Get to know him. Pray for him. Watch his attitudes. Does his obedience spring from a submissive heart, or is it motivated by a fear of man or the avoidance of conflict? Encourage him to take the risks that his temperament may naturally avoid, and don't give in to the temptation to shield him from the consequences when he does make a poor decision. Pray for him and encourage him as you see the fruits of the Spirit made evident in his life.

Parenting the Strong-Willed Child

Other children seem to arrive with an extra dose of determination! For those of us who thought we had it all together after the first child, this one completely destroys all our self-righteous delusions! It becomes much more obvious that we must continually seek God's wisdom and patience as we labor to lead this child into submission.

Persevere! Proverbs 29:15 encourages us to remember that "the rod and reproof give wisdom: but a child left to himself bringeth his mother to shame." Although this child may test you at every turn, leave you exhausted at the end of the day, and tempt you to discouragement or anger, your faithful and consistent discipline will be well-invested. Proverbs 29:17 states, "Correct thy son, and he shall give thee rest; yea, he shall give delight unto thy soul." Brought under discipline and submission, the determined child is a delight! God has a plan for that strong will! Appreciate this child's gift, and prayerfully train him to submit. (I'll bet the apostle Paul was a strong-willed child!)

Parenting the Rebellious Child

Because we are all born with a free will and an old sin nature, our parenting efforts may occasionally be rewarded with rebellion. The wise sayings of Proverbs acknowledge this painful state of affairs.

> "A foolish son is a grief to his father, and bitterness to her that bare him." (Proverbs 17:25)

> "...A wise son maketh a glad father: but a foolish son is the heaviness of his mother." (Proverbs 10:1)

We should expect that our children, the children of believing parents, will follow our Lord. Rejection of their training will not be the norm. A wise parent will certainly examine himself when a son or daughter resists his leadership and authority. He will humbly go to God in prayer. He will go to the mirror of God's Word and take an honest look at himself in light of God's truth and commands. He will seek the honest counsel and insights of godly friends and church leaders.

If you are dealing with a rebellious child, take time to prayerfully look at your own life. Are your own sinful attitudes contributing to the problem? Are you unloving, distant, hypocritical, preoccupied, indifferent, unreasonable, or too busy? Do you focus on rules, but neglect to balance them with mercy and grace? Are you inconsistent or unjust, disciplining according to your changing mood? Is it impossible to please you?

What are you teaching your children through your example? Do you honor the authorities over you? Do you cheerfully submit to God and to those He has placed over you?

The Westminster Larger Catechism, in addition to detailing the duties and sins of inferiors, also addresses the duties and sins of superiors. Prayerfully consider the teaching offered in the following questions and answers:

Q. 129. What is required of superiors towards their inferiors?
A. It is required of superiors, according to that power they receive from God, and that relation wherein they stand, to love, pray for, and bless their inferiors; to instruct, counsel, and admonish them; countenancing,

commending, and rewarding such as do well; and discountenancing, reproving, and chastising such as do ill; protecting, and providing for them all things necessary for soul and body: and by grave, wise, holy, and exemplary carriage, to procure glory to God, honour to themselves, and so to preserve that authority which God hath put upon them.

Q. 130. What are the sins of superiors?

A. The sins of superiors are, besides the neglect of the duties required of them, and inordinate seeking of themselves, their own glory, ease, profit, or pleasure; commanding things unlawful, or not in the power of inferiors to perform; counseling, encouraging, or favouring them in that which is evil; dissuading, discouraging, or discountenancing them in that which is good; correcting them unduly; careless exposing, or leaving them to wrong, temptation, and danger; provoking them to wrath; or any way dishonouring themselves, or lessening their authority, by an unjust, indiscreet, rigorous, or remiss behaviour.

No parent can look at God's Word and honestly claim he is without sin. We know that we all fall far short of the standard God has outlined for us. Ask God to reveal areas of sin to you. Seek forgiveness from Him and your children. Repent and draw on His wisdom that is readily available, and His grace that is all-sufficient. With God's help, obey Him.

We are all inadequate for the job of parenting. God gave Adam and Eve children after they had sinned. He chooses to give us children and the responsibilities of parenting in spite of our sin and shortcomings. He remembers that we are dust (Psalm 103:14), and He gives us His Holy Spirit to aid us. He blesses us with children, and causes us to grow in Him as we seek His wisdom, grace, and strength to raise those children for His glory.

Pray for your rebellious child. Only God can change his heart. "And I will give them one heart, and I will put a new spirit within you; and I will take the stony heart out of their flesh, and will give them an heart of flesh: that they may walk in my statutes, and keep mine ordinances, and do them: and they shall be my people, and I will be their God." (Ezekiel 11:19-20)

If your child is in rebellion, don't give up. Don't grow angry and combative. Don't withdraw, in shame, from the body of Christ. Acknowledge your need, and seek the prayers, counsel, and support of others. Examine your own heart, repent of sin, obey God as you train your children, and trust Him with the results.

"Except the LORD build the house, they labour in vain that build it: except the LORD keep the city, the watchman waketh but in vain." *(Psalm 127:1)*

I honor my parents by giving them:

All Due Reverence in Heart

God has put me under the authority of my parents. He commands me to fear them with respect and esteem. This reverence should not only be an outward display but a reverence of heart that encompasses my affections, my understanding, my will, my plans, my hidden thoughts, and my conscience.

Have I put my faith in Christ's death and resurrection as the only means of salvation?

"Jesus saith unto him, I am the way, the truth, and the life: no man cometh unto the Father, but by me." (John 14:6)

"For he hath made him to be sin for us, who knew no sin; that we might be made the righteousness of God in him." (2 Corinthians 5:21)

Do I truly fear God and seek, by His grace, to obey Him?

"And thou shalt love the Lord thy God with all thy heart, and with all thy soul, and with all thy mind, and with all thy strength: this is the first commandment. And the second is like, namely this, Thou shalt love thy neighbour as thyself. There is none other commandment greater than these." (Mark 12:30-31)

"Remember now thy Creator in the days of thy youth, while the evil days come not, nor the years draw nigh, when thou shalt say, I have no pleasure in them." (Ecclesiastes 12:1)

Have I put my faith in the righteousness of Christ as the only foundation for my obedience to God's Word? Do I realize that I will never be righteous in my own strength, but must rely on God's grace to enable me to live a life of obedience, and to forgive me when I fail?

"For by grace are ye saved through faith; and that not of yourselves: it is the gift of God: not of works, lest any man should boast. For we are his workmanship, created in Christ Jesus unto good works, which God hath before ordained that we should walk in them." (Ephesians 2:8-10)

"Thou therefore, my son, be strong in the grace that is in Christ Jesus." (2 Timothy 2:1)

"I can do all things through Christ which strengtheneth me." (Philippians 4:13)

"And he said unto me, My grace is sufficient for thee: for my strength is made perfect in weakness. Most gladly therefore will I rather glory in my infirmities, that the power of Christ may rest upon me." (2 Corinthians 12:9)

Is my goal in life to please God?

"For it is God which worketh in you both to will and to do of his good pleasure." (Philippians 2:13)

"Whether therefore ye eat, or drink, or whatsoever ye do, do all to the glory of God." (1 Corinthians 10:31)

"So then they that are in the flesh cannot please God." (Romans 8:8)

"Delight thyself also in the LORD; and he shall give thee the desires of thine heart." (Psalm 37:4)

Do I trust God with my life, acknowledging that He sovereignly knows what is best for me and my family?

"But now, O LORD, thou art our father; we are the clay, and thou our potter; and we all are the work of thy hand." (Isaiah 64:8)

"The LORD will perfect that which concerneth me: thy mercy, O LORD, endureth for ever: forsake not the works of thine own hands." (Psalm 138:8)

Is my faith in Christ demonstrated in a sincere desire to obey Him?

"And hereby we do know that we know him, if we keep his commandments." (1 John 2:3)

"And why call ye me, Lord, Lord, and do not the things which I say?" (Luke 6:46)

Do I recognize that I can please God and bring glory to Him by honoring and obeying my parents?

"Let your light so shine before men, that they may see your good works, and glorify your Father which is in heaven." (Matthew 5:16)

"Submit yourselves to every ordinance of man for the Lord's sake: whether it be to the king, as supreme; or unto governors, as unto them that are sent by him for the punishment of evildoers, and for the praise of them that do well. For so is the will of God, that with well doing ye may put to silence the ignorance of foolish men." (1 Peter 2:13-15)

"Children, obey your parents in all things: for this is well pleasing unto the Lord." (Colossians 3:20)

Do I believe and quietly rest in the fact that God, in His loving sovereignty, has placed my parents over me?

"Let every soul be subject unto the higher powers. For there is no power but of God: the powers that be are ordained of God." (Romans 13:1)

Do I recognize that God will bless me through the covenantal relationship I share with my parents?

"But the mercy of the LORD is from everlasting to everlasting upon them that fear him, and his righteousness unto children's children." (Psalm 103:17)

"The just man walketh in his integrity: his children are blessed after him." (Proverbs 20:7)

"For the promise is unto you, and to your children, and to all that are afar off, even as many as the Lord our God shall call." (Acts 2:39)

"Honour thy father and mother; (which is the first commandment with promise ;) that it may be well with thee, and thou mayest live long on the earth." (Ephesians 6:2-3)

Do my parents have my heart? Do I trust them as God uses them to lead me, working all things out for my ultimate good?

"My son, give me thine heart. . ." (Proverbs 23:26a)

"And he shall turn the heart of the fathers to the children, and the heart of the children to their fathers, lest I come and smite the earth with a curse." (Malachi 4:6)

"For I know the thoughts that I think toward you, saith the LORD, thoughts of peace, and not of evil, to give you an expected end." (Jeremiah 29:11)

Are my thoughts and attitudes, as well as my actions, toward my parents ones of trust and reverence?

". . .For the LORD seeth not as man seeth; for man looketh on the outward appearance, but the LORD looketh on the heart." (1 Samuel 16:7b)

"Examine me, O LORD, and prove me; try my reins and my heart." (Psalm 26:2)

"My son, give me thine heart, and let thine eyes observe my ways." (Proverbs 23:26)

"Not with eyeservice, as menpleasers; but as the servants of Christ, doing the will of God from the heart." (Ephesians 6:6)

Do I recognize that God has given me as a blessing to my parents?

"Lo, children are an heritage of the LORD: and the fruit of the womb is his reward." (Psalm 127:3)

"Blessed is every one that feareth the LORD; that walketh in his ways. For thou shalt eat the labour of thine hands: happy shalt thou be, and it shall be well with thee. Thy wife shall be as a fruitful vine by the sides of thine house: thy children like olive plants round about thy table." (Psalm 128:1-3)

Am I bringing joy and blessing to my parents?

"My son, be wise, and make my heart glad, that I may answer him that reproacheth me." (Proverbs 27:11)

"My son, if thine heart be wise, my heart shall rejoice, even mine. Yea, my reins shall rejoice, when thy lips speak right things." (Proverbs 23:15-16)

"The father of the righteous shall greatly rejoice: and he that begetteth a wise child shall have joy of him. Thy father and thy mother shall be glad, and she that bare thee shall rejoice." (Proverbs 23:24-25)

Do I desire to please my parents and to joyfully advance the goals they have for me and for our family?

"Jesus saith unto them, My meat is to do the will of him that sent me, and to finish his work." (John 4:34)

"Let every one of us please his neighbour for his good to edification." (Romans 15:2)

"As arrows are in the hand of a mighty man; so are children of the youth. Happy is the man that hath his quiver full of them: they shall not be ashamed, but they shall speak with the enemies in the gate."(Psalm 127:4-5)

Does God's Word govern my relationship with my parents? Do I study the Bible and humbly submit to it?

"The entrance of thy words giveth light; it giveth understanding unto the simple." (Psalm 119:130)

"Teach me to do thy will; for thou art my God: thy spirit is good; lead me into the land of uprightness." (Psalm 143:10)

"I delight to do thy will, O my God: yea, thy law is within my heart." (Psalm 40:8)

"With my whole heart have I sought thee: O let me not wander from thy commandments. Thy word have I hid in mine heart, that I might not sin against thee." (Psalm 119:10-11)

"But his delight is in the law of the LORD; and in his law doth he meditate day and night. And he shall be like a tree planted by the rivers of water, that bringeth forth his fruit in his season; his leaf also shall not wither; and whatsoever he doeth shall prosper." (Psalm 1:2-3)

Do I seek to submit to my parents in the same way that Jesus submitted to His Father?

"Take my yoke upon you, and learn of me; for I am meek and lowly in heart: and ye shall find rest unto your souls." (Matthew 11:29)

"Saying, Father, if thou be willing, remove this cup from me: nevertheless not my will, but thine, be done." (Luke 22:42)

"And he that sent me is with me: the Father hath not left me alone; for I do always those things that please him." (John 8:29)

"Let this mind be in you, which was also in Christ Jesus: who, being in the form of God, thought it not robbery to be equal with God: but made himself of no reputation, and took upon him the form of a servant, and was made in the likeness of men: and being found in fashion as a man, he humbled himself, and became obedient unto death, even the death of the cross." (Philippians 2:5-8)

"He that saith he abideth in him ought himself also so to walk, even as he walked." (1 John 2:6)

Is my relationship with my parents a higher priority to me than my relationships with my friends?

"My son, give me thine heart, and let thine eyes observe my ways." (Proverbs 23:26)

"Hearken unto thy father that begat thee, and despise not thy mother when she is old." (Proverbs 23:22)

Does my face reflect the respect that I have for my parents?

"A merry heart maketh a cheerful countenance: but by sorrow of the heart the spirit is broken." (Proverbs 15:13)

"Who is as the wise man? and who knoweth the interpretation of a thing? a man's wisdom maketh his face to shine, and the boldness of his face shall be changed." (Ecclesiastes 8:1)

Because of my desire to obey God, am I choosing to honor my parents' authority over me (even when their actions, or lack of them, may be sinful)?

"Submitting yourselves one to another in the fear of God . . ." (Ephesians 5:21)

"Servants, be subject to your masters with all fear; not only to the good and gentle, but also to the froward. For this is thankworthy, if a man for conscience toward God endure grief, suffering wrongfully." (1 Peter 2:18-19)

"Delight thyself also in the LORD; and he shall give thee the desires of thine heart. Commit thy way unto the LORD; trust also in him; and he shall bring it to pass. And he shall bring forth thy righteousness as the light, and thy judgment as the noonday. Rest in the LORD, and wait patiently for him: fret not thyself because of him who prospereth in his way, because of the man who bringeth wicked devices to pass. Cease from anger, and forsake wrath: fret not thyself in any wise to do evil." (Psalm 37:4-8)

"But as for you, ye thought evil against me; but God meant it unto good, to bring to pass, as it is this day, to save much people alive." (Genesis 50:20)

Do I put my trust in God when my parents seem to fail me?

"Come unto me, all ye that labour and are heavy laden, and I will give you rest. Take my yoke upon you, and learn of me; for I am meek and lowly in heart: and ye shall find rest unto your souls. For my yoke is easy, and my burden is light." (Matthew 11:28-30).

"The LORD is on my side; I will not fear: what can man do unto me?" (Psalm 118:6)

"For I know the thoughts that I think toward you, saith the LORD, thoughts of peace, and not of evil, to give you an expected end." (Jeremiah 29:11)

I honor my parents by giving them:
All Due Reverence in Word

Because God has put me under the authority of my parents and requires my reverence and obedience, He also commands that I demonstrate my respect and esteem with my words, my willingness to communicate clearly and honestly, and my unfailing honoring of the commitments I make.

Do the words I speak to my parents reflect a quiet trust in God as the sovereign controller of all that takes place in my life?

"A good man out of the good treasure of his heart bringeth forth that which is good; and an evil man out of the evil treasure of his heart bringeth forth that which is evil: for of the abundance of the heart his mouth speaketh." (Luke 6:45)

Do the words I speak to my parents reflect reverence for them as God's gracious gift and appointed authority over me?

". . . for out of the abundance of the heart the mouth speaketh." (Matthew 12:34b)

"For by thy words thou shalt be justified, and by thy words thou shalt be condemned." (Matthew 12:37)

"There is one who speaks like the piercings of a sword, but the tongue of the wise promotes health." (Proverbs 12:18, NKJV)

Do I speak to my parents with a respectful tone of voice that is pleasant and friendly?

"Render therefore to all their dues: tribute to whom tribute is due; custom to whom custom; fear to whom fear; honour to whom honour." (Romans 13:7)

"A wholesome tongue is a tree of life: but perverseness therein is a breach in the spirit." (Proverbs 15:4)

"He that loveth pureness of heart, for the grace of his lips the king shall be his friend." (Proverbs 22:11)

Do I pray for wisdom and weigh my words carefully when speaking to my parents?

"Set a watch, O LORD, before my mouth; keep the door of my lips." (Psalm 141:3)

"The words of a wise man's mouth are gracious; but the lips of a fool will swallow up himself." (Ecclesiastes 10:12)

"The lips of the righteous know what is acceptable: but the mouth of the wicked speaketh frowardness." (Proverbs 10:32)

"The heart of the righteous studieth to answer: but the mouth of the wicked poureth out evil things." (Proverbs 15:28)

"Let your speech be alway with grace, seasoned with salt, that ye may know how ye ought to answer every man." (Colossians 4:6)

Do I show respect to my parents by being patient, listening carefully, and not interrupting or voicing my own thoughts and opinions before they have finished speaking?

"Seest thou a man that is hasty in his words? there is more hope of a fool than of him." (Proverbs 29:20)

"Whoso keepeth his mouth and his tongue keepeth his soul from troubles." (Proverbs 21:23)

"A man hath joy by the answer of his mouth: and a word spoken in due season, how good is it!" (Proverbs 15:23)

"Wherefore, my beloved brethren, let every man be swift to hear, slow to speak, slow to wrath." (James 1:19)

"A fool uttereth all his mind: but a wise man keepeth it in till afterwards." (Proverbs 29:11)

Will I, without shame, be able to give an account to God for every word I have spoken to my parents?

"But I say unto you, That every idle word that men shall speak, they shall give account thereof in the day of judgment. For by thy words thou shalt be justified, and by thy words thou shalt be condemned." (Matthew 12:36-37)

"In the multitude of words there wanteth not sin: but he that refraineth his lips is wise." (Proverbs 10:19)

Do I show respect and honor when speaking of my parents to others?

"The Lord knoweth how to deliver the godly out of temptations, and to reserve the unjust unto the day of judgment to be punished: but chiefly them that walk after the flesh in the lust of uncleanness, and despise government. Presumptuous are they, selfwilled, they are not afraid to speak evil of dignities."(2 Peter 2:9-10)

"Debate thy cause with thy neighbour himself; and discover not a secret to another: Lest he that heareth it put thee to shame, and thine infamy turn not away." (Proverbs 25:9-10)

Do I respect my parents by not revealing private information about them and our family to others?

"A talebearer revealeth secrets: but he that is of a faithful spirit concealeth the matter." (Proverbs 11:13)

"He that goeth about as a talebearer revealeth secrets: therefore meddle not with him that flattereth with his lips." (Proverbs 20:19)

Do I seek to minister to my parents with my words, building them up, thanking them for their leadership and sacrifice, encouraging them, and asking for ways to help them?

"Let us therefore follow after the things which make for peace, and things wherewith one may edify another." (Romans 14:19)

"Let no corrupt communication proceed out of your mouth, but that which is good to the use of edifying, that it may minister grace unto the hearers." (Ephesians 4:29)

"Heaviness in the heart of man maketh it stoop: but a good word maketh it glad." (Proverbs 12:25)

"Pleasant words are as an honeycomb, sweet to the soul, and health to the bones." (Proverbs 16:24)

"Wherefore comfort yourselves together, and edify one another, even as also ye do." (1 Thessalonians 5:11)

"Even as the Son of man came not to be ministered unto, but to minister, and to give his life a ransom for many." (Matthew 20:28)

Do I respond with respect to my parents' words and instructions so they know that I am listening?

"Can two walk together, except they be agreed?" (Amos 3:3)

"A man hath joy by the answer of his mouth: and a word spoken in due season, how good is it!" (Proverbs 15:23)

"Let your speech be alway with grace, seasoned with salt, that ye may know how ye ought to answer every man." (Colossians 4:6)

"Righteous lips are the delight of kings; and they love him that speaketh right." (Proverbs 16:13)

Do I keep my word with my parents? Do I honor the promises and commitments that I have made?

"That which is gone out of thy lips thou shalt keep and perform; even a freewill offering, according as thou hast vowed unto the LORD thy God, which thou hast promised with thy mouth." (Deuteronomy 23:23)

"Whoso boasteth himself of a false gift is like clouds and wind without rain." (Proverbs 25:14)

"LORD, who shall abide in thy tabernacle? who shall dwell in thy holy hill? . . . He that sweareth to his own hurt, and changeth not. . . . He that doeth these things shall never be moved." (Psalm 15:1, 4b, 5b)

"But let your communication be, Yea, yea; Nay, nay: for whatsoever is more than these cometh of evil." (Matthew 5:37)

Do I talk to my parents as much as they would like me to? Do I willingly converse with them, respectfully sharing my thoughts and feelings, answering their questions, building our relationship together?

"The lips of the righteous know what is acceptable: but the mouth of the wicked speaketh frowardness." (Proverbs 10:32)

"The lips of the wise disperse knowledge: but the heart of the foolish doeth not so." (Proverbs 15:7)

"Render therefore to all their dues: tribute to whom tribute is due; custom to whom custom; fear to whom fear; honour to whom honour. Owe no man any thing, but to love one another: for he that loveth another hath fulfilled the law." (Romans 13:7-8)

Am I honest with my parents, willingly offering them all the information they, as my parents, are entitled to? Am I careful not to withhold information or phrase statements in a manner that could be misinterpreted? Are my words always clearly true?

"Providing for honest things, not only in the sight of the Lord, but also in the sight of men." (2 Corinthians 8:21)

"Behold, thou desirest truth in the inward parts: and in the hidden part thou shalt make me to know wisdom." (Psalm 51:6)

"Righteous lips are the delight of kings; and they love him that speaketh right." (Proverbs 16:13)

"Wherefore putting away lying, speak every man truth with his neighbour: for we are members one of another." (Ephesians 4:25)

Do I speak sincere words to my parents, refraining from the use of flattery or dishonesty to influence them?

"LORD, who shall abide in thy tabernacle? who shall dwell in thy holy hill? He that walketh uprightly, and worketh righteousness, and speaketh the truth in his heart." (Psalm 15:1-2)

"Nevertheless they did flatter him with their mouth, and they lied unto him with their tongues. For their heart was not right with him, neither were they steadfast in his covenant." (Psalm 78:36-37)

"A double minded man is unstable in all his ways." (James 1:8)

Do my words always reflect a quiet submission to my parents' authority and decisions, even when I disagree with them? Do I refrain from arguing, whining, criticizing, or grumbling?

"In the multitude of words there wanteth not sin: but he that refraineth his lips is wise." (Proverbs 10:19)

"He that hath knowledge spareth his words: and a man of understanding is of an excellent spirit." (Proverbs 17:27)

"Do all things without murmurings and disputings." (Philippians 2:14)

"A soft answer turneth away wrath: but grievous words stir up anger." (Proverbs 15:1)

"The beginning of strife is as when one letteth out water: therefore leave off contention, before it be meddled with." (Proverbs 17:14)

When I believe there is a biblically sound reason to further discuss a decision my parents have made, do I first express my willingness to obey and then ask their permission to appeal? With their approval, do I then offer only new or additional information they may need to wisely make their decision?

"Let your speech be alway with grace, seasoned with salt, that ye may know how ye ought to answer every man." (Colossians 4:6)

"The words of wise men are heard in quiet more than the cry of him that ruleth among fools." (Ecclesiastes 9:17)

"The tongue of the wise useth knowledge aright: but the mouth of fools poureth out foolishness." (Proverbs 15:2)

"The wise in heart shall be called prudent: and the sweetness of the lips increaseth learning." (Proverbs 16:21)

Do I exercise patience and self-control, praying and then waiting for the right time and place to respectfully discuss differences with my parents?

"To every thing there is a season, and a time to every purpose under the heaven: a time to rend, and a time to sew; a time to keep silence, and a time to speak." (Ecclesiastes 3:1 and 7)

"The heart of the righteous studieth to answer: but the mouth of the wicked poureth out evil things." (Proverbs 15:28)

"The heart of the wise teacheth his mouth, and addeth learning to his lips." (Proverbs 16:23)

"He that keepeth his mouth keepeth his life: but he that openeth wide his lips shall have destruction." (Proverbs 13:3)

"A fool uttereth all his mind: but a wise man keepeth it in till afterwards." (Proverbs 29:11)

"Go not forth hastily to strive, lest thou know not what to do in the end thereof, when thy neighbour hath put thee to shame." (Proverbs 25:8)

After respectfully appealing to my parents, do I quietly trust God to lead me through their final decisions and actions, even when I disagree with them?

"Let every soul be subject unto the higher powers. For there is no power but of God: the powers that be are ordained of God. Whosoever therefore resisteth the power, resisteth the ordinance of God: and they that resist shall receive to themselves damnation. For rulers are not a terror to good works, but to the evil. Wilt thou then not be afraid of the power? Do that which is good, and thou shalt have praise of the same: for he is the minister of God to thee for good. But if thou do that which is evil, be afraid; for he beareth not the sword in vain: for he is the minister of God, a revenger to execute wrath upon him that doeth evil. Wherefore ye must needs be subject, not only for wrath, but also for conscience sake." (Romans 13:1-5)

"For I know the thoughts that I think toward you, saith the LORD, thoughts of peace, and not of evil, to give you an expected end." (Jeremiah 29:11)

"Do all things without murmurings and disputings." (Philippians 2:14)

"And the fruit of righteousness is sown in peace of them that make peace." (James 3:18)

Do I quickly repent and ask forgiveness of my parents when I have sinned against them?

"Therefore if thou bring thy gift to the altar, and there rememberest that thy brother hath ought against thee; leave there thy gift before the altar, and go thy way; first be reconciled to thy brother, and then come and offer thy gift. (Matthew 5:23-24)

"Confess your faults one to another, and pray one for another, that ye may be healed. The effectual fervent prayer of a righteous man availeth much." (James 5:16)

Do my words show reverence for my parents as God's appointed heads over me, even when they have failed, sinned, or deeply wronged me?

"Let all bitterness, and wrath, and anger, and clamour, and evil speaking, be put away from you, with all malice. And be ye kind one to another, tenderhearted, forgiving one another, even as God for Christ's sake hath forgiven you." (Ephesians 4:31-32)

"A word fitly spoken is like apples of gold in pictures of silver." (Proverbs 25:11)

"The heart of the wise teacheth his mouth, and addeth learning to his lips." (Proverbs 16:23)

I honor my parents by giving them:

All Due Reverence in Behavior

The respect and esteem I am commanded to have for my parents must be proven with my actions. My facial expressions, bodily gestures, manners, dress, and actions must all communicate a reverence for my parents as God's representative authorities. I must honor them with humble, quick, and cheerful obedience, and with careful attentiveness to their needs and desires.

Is my sincere reverence for God displayed in actions that demonstrate a sincere and godly reverence for my parents?

"Let your light so shine before men, that they may see your good works, and glorify your Father which is in heaven." (Matthew 5:16)

"Even a child is known by his doings, whether his work be pure, and whether it be right." (Proverbs 20:11)

"Wherefore by their fruits ye shall know them." (Matthew 7:20)

Do I spend time with my parents, nurturing a strong and loving relationship with them?

"For where your treasure is, there will your heart be also." (Matthew 6:21)

"My little children, let us not love in word, neither in tongue; but in deed and in truth." (1 John 3:18)

Do I invest thought, time, and energy in pleasing my parents? Do I put my parents' needs, goals, and wishes before my own?

"Greater love hath no man than this, that a man lay down his life for his friends." (John 15:13)

"Let no man seek his own, but every man another's wealth." (1 Corinthians 10:24)

"Be kindly affectioned one to another with brotherly love; in honour preferring one another." (Romans 12:10)

"Even as the Son of man came not to be ministered unto, but to minister, and to give his life a ransom for many." (Matthew 20:28)

Do I seek to please my parents by deferring to their preferences in matters of dress, hairstyle, music, and speech? Do I refrain from habits that displease them?

"Let nothing be done through strife or vainglory; but in lowliness of mind let each esteem other better than themselves." (Philippians 2:3)

"Be kindly affectioned one to another with brotherly love; in honour preferring one another." (Romans 12:10)

"If it be possible, as much as lieth in you, live peaceably with all men." (Romans 12:18)

"I therefore, the prisoner of the Lord, beseech you that ye walk worthy of the vocation wherewith ye are called, with all lowliness and meekness, with longsuffering, forbearing one another in love." (Ephesians 4:1-2)

Do my actions and manners show kindness and a proper esteem and honor for my parents? Do I perform acts of courtesy and service that honor their position as my parents?

"And we beseech you, brethren, to know them which labour among you, and are over you in the Lord, and admonish you; and to esteem them very highly in love for their work's sake. And be at peace among yourselves." (1 Thessalonians 5:12-13)

"Thou shalt rise up before the hoary head, and honour the face of the old man, and fear thy God: I am the LORD." (Leviticus 19:32)

"And one of you say unto them, Depart in peace, be ye warmed and filled; notwithstanding ye give them not those things which are needful to the body; what doth it profit? Even so faith, if it hath not works, is dead, being alone." (James 2:16-17)

Do I honor my parents by exercising patience and self-control as God has commanded in my relationship with them?

"He that is slow to anger is better than the mighty; and he that ruleth his spirit than he that taketh a city." (Proverbs 16:32)

"A wrathful man stirreth up strife: but he that is slow to anger appeaseth strife." (Proverbs 15:18)

"But the fruit of the Spirit is love, joy, peace, longsuffering, gentleness, goodness, faith, meekness, temperance: against such there is no law." (Galatians 5:22-23)

Do I actively listen, giving my parents my undivided attention when they speak?

"Wherefore, my beloved brethren, let every man be swift to hear, slow to speak, slow to wrath." (James 1:19)

"My son, attend to my words; incline thine ear unto my sayings." (Proverbs 4:20)

"Bow down thine ear, and hear the words of the wise, and apply thine heart unto my knowledge." (Proverbs 22:17)

Do I do what I know my parents would want me to do, even when they are not with me, or when they have not clearly specified their wishes in a particular situation?

"Therefore to him that knoweth to do good, and doeth it not, to him it is sin." (James 4:17)

"I the LORD search the heart, I try the reins, even to give every man according to his ways, and according to the fruit of his doings." (Jeremiah 17:10)

Do my facial expressions and bodily gestures show honor for my parents?

"A man's wisdom maketh his face to shine, and the boldness of his face shall be changed." (Ecclesiastes 8:1b)

"The shew of their countenance doth witness against them; and they declare their sin as Sodom, they hide it not. Woe unto their soul! for they have rewarded evil unto themselves." (Isaiah 3:9)

"These six things doth the LORD hate: yea, seven are an abomination unto him: a proud look, a lying tongue, and hands that shed innocent blood . . ." (Proverbs 6:16-17)

Do I treat my parents the same way at home as I do in public?

"Though I speak with the tongues of men and of angels, and have not charity, I am become as sounding brass, or a tinkling cymbal." (1 Corinthians 13:1)

"Take heed that ye do not your alms before men, to be seen of them: otherwise ye have no reward of your Father which is in heaven. Therefore when thou doest thine alms, do not sound a trumpet before thee, as the hypocrites do in the synagogues and in the streets, that they may have glory of men. Verily I say unto you, They have their reward. But when thou doest alms, let not thy left hand know what thy right hand doeth: that thine alms may be in secret: and thy Father which seeth in secret himself shall reward thee openly. (Matthew 6:1-4)

Do I demonstrate my trust in God by continuing to show respect and honor to my parents, even if they have sinned against me?

"Wherein ye greatly rejoice, though now for a season, if need be, ye are in heaviness through manifold temptations: That the trial of your faith, being much more precious than of gold that perisheth, though it be tried with fire, might be found unto praise and honour and glory at the appearing of Jesus Christ." (1 Peter 1:6-7)

"For what glory is it, if, when ye be buffeted for your faults, ye shall take it patiently? but if, when ye do well, and suffer for it, ye take it patiently, this is acceptable with God. For even hereunto were ye called: because Christ also suffered for us, leaving us an example, that ye should follow his steps: who did no sin, neither was guile found in his mouth: who, when he was reviled, reviled not again; when he suffered, he threatened not; but committed himself to him that judgeth righteously." (1 Peter 2:20-23)

If my parents refuse to repent after I respectfully appeal to them regarding serious sin against me or other members of my family, have I sought the counsel and protection of the authorities in my church?

"Moreover if thy brother shall trespass against thee, go and tell him his fault between thee and him alone: if he shall hear thee, thou hast gained thy brother. But if he will not hear thee, then take with thee one or two more, that in the mouth of two or three witnesses every word may be established. And if he shall neglect to hear them, tell it unto the church: but if he neglect to hear the church, let him be unto thee as an heathen man and a publican." (Matthew 18:15-17)

I honor my parents through:

Prayer

My life should be filled with prayer for my parents. I must honor them by regularly appealing to God on their behalf. I must pray for His hand of blessing in their lives, for strength and wisdom as they serve Him in their various God-given callings, for His mercy and grace as they struggle against sin, and for His convicting Holy Spirit when they act against His Word. I must pray for God to enable me to be a source of grace, blessing, and encouragement in their lives.

Do I earnestly pray that my parents will grow in wisdom and obedience to God and His Word?

"Wherefore I also, after I heard of your faith in the Lord Jesus, and love unto all the saints, cease not to give thanks for you, making mention of you in my prayers; that the God of our Lord Jesus Christ, the Father of glory, may give unto you the spirit of wisdom and revelation in the knowledge of him: the eyes of your understanding being enlightened; that ye may know what is the hope of his calling, and what the riches of the glory of his inheritance in the saints, and what is the exceeding greatness of his power to usward who believe, according to the working of his mighty power." (Ephesians 1:15-19)

"For this cause we also, since the day we heard it, do not cease to pray for you, and to desire that ye might be filled with the knowledge of his will in all wisdom and spiritual understanding; that ye might walk worthy of the Lord unto all pleasing, being fruitful in every good work, and increasing in the knowledge of God; strengthened with all might, according to his glorious power, unto all patience and longsuffering with joyfulness; giving thanks unto the Father, which hath made us meet to be partakers of the inheritance of the saints in light." (Colossians 1:9-12)

Do I pray that my parents will continually grow in their love for each other?

"Therefore shall a man leave his father and his mother, and shall cleave unto his wife: and they shall be one flesh." (Genesis 2:24)

"Therefore as the church is subject unto Christ, so let the wives be to their own husbands in every thing. Husbands, love your wives, even as Christ also loved the church, and gave himself for it." (Ephesians 5:24-25)

Do I pray that God will grant my parents His wisdom as they seek to obediently love and train me and my siblings?

"Moreover as for me, God forbid that I should sin against the LORD in ceasing to pray for you." (1 Samuel 12:23a)

"I exhort therefore, that, first of all, supplications, prayers, intercessions, and giving of thanks, be made for all men; for kings, and for all that are in authority; that we may lead a quiet and peaceable life in all godliness and honesty." (1 Timothy 2:1-2)

"That they may offer sacrifices of sweet savours unto the God of heaven, and pray for the life of the king, and of his sons." (Ezra 6:10)

"And this I pray, that your love may abound yet more and more in knowledge and in all judgment." (Philippians 1:9)

Do I pray for my parents and their relationship with each of the children in our family?

"And he shall turn the heart of the fathers to the children, and the heart of the children to their fathers, lest I come and smite the earth with a curse." (Malachi 4:6)

"The father of the righteous shall greatly rejoice: and he that begetteth a wise child shall have joy of him. Thy father and thy mother shall be glad, and she that bare thee shall rejoice. My son, give me thine heart, and let thine eyes observe my ways." (Proverbs 23:24-26)

Do I pray for my parents when I know they are going through times of testing and hardship?

"For we have not an high priest which cannot be touched with the feeling of our infirmities; but was in all points tempted like as we are, yet without sin. Let us therefore come boldly unto the throne of grace, that we may obtain mercy, and find grace to help in time of need." (Hebrews 4:15-16)

"Be careful for nothing; but in every thing by prayer and supplication with thanksgiving let your requests be made known unto God." (Philippians 4:6)

"Rejoicing in hope; patient in tribulation; continuing instant in prayer. . ." (Romans 12:12)

"Bear ye one another's burdens, and so fulfil the law of Christ." (Galatians 6:2)

Do I pray for my parents to be blessed with physical strength and good health?

"Beloved, I wish above all things that thou mayest prosper and be in health, even as thy soul prospereth." (3 John 2)

"The LORD will give strength unto his people; the LORD will bless his people with peace." (Psalm 29:11)

Do I pray for God to bless the relationship I share with my parents – that we will be of one mind, and that I will be a blessing and encouragement to them while they direct, counsel, and provide for me?

"But to do good and to communicate forget not: for with such sacrifices God is well pleased. Obey them that have the rule over you, and submit yourselves: for they watch for your souls, as they that must give account, that they may do it with joy, and not with grief: for that is unprofitable for you." (Heb 13:16-17)

Do I pray for a reverent heart and submissive response to my parents' leadership and instruction?

"Delight thyself also in the LORD; and he shall give thee the desires of thine heart. Commit thy way unto the LORD; trust also in him; and he shall bring it to pass." (Psalm 37:4-5)

"Examine me, O LORD, and prove me; try my reins and my heart." (Psalm 26:2)

"Search me, O God, and know my heart: try me, and know my thoughts: and see if there be any wicked way in me, and lead me in the way everlasting." (Psalm 139:23-24)

"Teach me to do thy will; for thou art my God: thy spirit is good; lead me into the land of uprightness." (Psalm 143:10)

Do I pray for my parent when he or she has offended me, or do I criticize and harbor bitterness or anger?

"Grudge not one against another, brethren, lest ye be condemned: behold, the judge standeth before the door." (James 5:9)

"Not rendering evil for evil, or railing for railing: but contrariwise blessing; knowing that ye are thereunto called, that ye should inherit a blessing." (1 Peter 3:9)

"And when ye stand praying, forgive, if ye have ought against any: that your Father also which is in heaven may forgive you your trespasses." (Mark 11:25)

When one of my parents is in sin or when I believe he or she is making an unwise or unjust decision, do I humbly entreat him or her, and then earnestly, patiently, and quietly pray for God to lead them according to His Word?

"Pray for us: for we trust we have a good conscience, in all things willing to live honestly."(Hebrews 13:18)

"Call unto me, and I will answer thee, and show thee great and mighty things, which thou knowest not." (Jeremiah 33:3)

"The king's heart is in the hand of the LORD, as the rivers of water: he turneth it whithersoever he will." (Proverbs 21:1)

"The LORD shall fight for you, and ye shall hold your peace." (Exodus 14:14)

I honor my parents with:

Thanksgiving

If I am truly honoring my parents as God's appointed authorities over me, I will have a deep sense of gratitude for them and their work in my life. I will thank God for His provision, protection, and guidance as it is demonstrated through my parents. With words and actions, I will thank my parents for their love and sacrifice.

Do I know God and thank Him for His saving grace, His sovereign wisdom, His unchanging justice, His unending love?

"Sing unto the LORD, O ye saints of his, and give thanks at the remembrance of his holiness." (Psalm 30:4)

"Thanks be unto God for his unspeakable gift." (2 Corinthians 9:15)

"Bless the LORD, O my soul: and all that is within me, bless his holy name. Bless the LORD, O my soul, and forget not all his benefits: who forgiveth all thine iniquities; who healeth all thy diseases; who redeemeth thy life from destruction; who crowneth thee with lovingkindness and tender mercies; who satisfieth thy mouth with good things; so that thy youth is renewed like the eagle's." (Psalm 103:1-5)

Am I seeking satisfaction in life from God or am I seeking it from my family, friends, possessions, reputation, etc.?

"For he satisfieth the longing soul, and filleth the hungry soul with goodness." (Psalm 107:9)

"As for me, I will behold thy face in righteousness: I shall be satisfied, when I awake, with thy likeness." (Psalm 17:15)

"They soon forgat his works; they waited not for his counsel: but lusted exceedingly in the wilderness, and tempted God in the desert. And he gave them their request; but sent leanness into their soul." (Psalm 106:13-15)

Do I trust God with my life? Do I thank Him for all circumstances, knowing that He knows what is best for me?

"In every thing give thanks: for this is the will of God in Christ Jesus concerning you." (1 Thessalonians 5:18)

"I will sing unto the LORD, because he hath dealt bountifully with me." (Psalm 13:6)

"Blessed be the Lord, who daily loadeth us with benefits, even the God of our salvation. Selah." (Psalm 68:19)

Am I content with what God, in His goodness, has chosen to give me (i.e., home, possessions, parents, friendships, circumstances)? Do I think I deserve more than He has given?

"And he said unto them, Take heed, and beware of covetousness: for a man's life consisteth not in the abundance of the things which he possesseth." (Luke 12:15)

"It is of the LORD'S mercies that we are not consumed, because his compassions fail not. They are new every morning: great is thy faithfulness." (Lamentations 3:22-23)

"Not that I speak in respect of want: for I have learned, in whatsoever state I am, therewith to be content." (Philippians 4:11)

"But godliness with contentment is great gain. For we brought nothing into this world, and it is certain we can carry nothing out. And having food and raiment let us be therewith content." (1 Timothy 6:6-8)

Do I refuse to compare my parents and circumstances unfavorably with those of others?

"Better is the sight of the eyes than the wandering of the desire: this is also vanity and vexation of spirit." (Ecclesiastes 6:9)

"Thou shalt not covet thy neighbour's house, thou shalt not covet thy neighbour's wife, nor his manservant, nor his maidservant, nor his ox, nor his ass, nor any thing that is thy neighbour's." (Exodus 20:17)

"Let your conversation be without covetousness; and be content with such things as ye have: for he hath said, I will never leave thee, nor forsake thee." (Hebrews 13:5)

Do I avoid conversations, friendships, reading material, TV programs, etc. that could lead me to be discontent with my parents? Do I actively pursue those things which encourage contentedness and faithfulness?

"Incline my heart unto thy testimonies, and not to covetousness." (Psalm 119:36)

"I will set no wicked thing before mine eyes: I hate the work of them that turn aside; it shall not cleave to me." (Psalm 101:3)

"And be not conformed to this world: but be ye transformed by the renewing of your mind, that ye may prove what is that good, and acceptable, and perfect, will of God." (Romans 12:2)

"Blessed is the man that walketh not in the counsel of the ungodly, nor standeth in the way of sinners, nor sitteth in the seat of the scornful. But his delight is in the law of the LORD; and in his law doth he meditate day and night." (Psalm 1:1-2)

"I am a companion of all them that fear thee, and of them that keep thy precepts." (Psalm 119:63)

"Go from the presence of a foolish man, when thou perceivest not in him the lips of knowledge." (Proverbs 14:7)

Do I thank God for my parents and for what He is accomplishing in my life through them?

"I thank my God upon every remembrance of you, always in every prayer of mine for you all making request with joy." (Philippians 1:3-4)

"I exhort therefore, that, first of all, supplications, prayers, intercessions, and giving of thanks, be made for all men; for kings, and for all that are in authority; that we may lead a quiet and peaceable life in all godliness and honesty." (1 Timothy 2:1-2)

Have I verbally acknowledged to my parents their right to exercise authority over me, and have I thanked them for exercising that responsibility in my life?

"For rulers are not a terror to good works, but to the evil. Wilt thou then not be afraid of the power? Do that which is good, and thou shalt have praise of the same: for he is the minister of God to thee for good." (Romans 13:3-4a)

"Pleasant words are as an honeycomb, sweet to the soul, and health to the bones." (Proverbs 16:24)

"A word fitly spoken is like apples of gold in pictures of silver." (Proverbs 25:11)

Do I verbally express my gratitude for the many acts of love and service that my parents perform for me? Do I thank them for the daily blessings of meals, clothes, transportation, etc.? Do they know I appreciate them?

"In every thing give thanks: for this is the will of God in Christ Jesus concerning you." (1 Thessalonians 5:18)

Am I thankful for my parents' love for me?

"We give thanks to God always for you all, making mention of you in our prayers: remembering without ceasing your work of faith, and labour of love, and patience of hope in our Lord Jesus Christ, in the sight of God and our Father." (1 Thessalonians 1:2-3)

Do I love my parents?

"Render therefore to all their dues: tribute to whom tribute is due; custom to whom custom; fear to whom fear; honour to whom honour. Owe no man any thing, but to love one another: for he that loveth another hath fulfilled the law." (Romans 13:7-8)

"And this commandment have we from him, that he who loveth God love his brother also." (1 John 4:21)

Am I thankful for my parents' counsel and correction?

"Foolishness is bound in the heart of a child; but the rod of correction shall drive it far from him." (Proverbs 22:15)

"My son, despise not the chastening of the LORD; neither be weary of his correction: for whom the LORD loveth he correcteth; even as a father the son in whom he delighteth." (Proverbs 3:11-12)

"If ye endure chastening, God dealeth with you as with sons; for what son is he whom the father chasteneth not? But if ye be without chastisement, whereof all are partakers, then are ye bastards, and not sons." (Hebrews 12:7-8)

"He that rebuketh a man afterwards shall find more favour than he that flattereth with the tongue." (Proverbs 28:23)

Do I seek to bless my parents, demonstrating my thankfulness to them with my actions?

"My little children, let us not love in word, neither in tongue; but in deed and in truth." (1 John 3:18)

"Withhold not good from them to whom it is due, when it is in the power of thine hand to do it." (Proverbs 3:27)

"Even so faith, if it hath not works, is dead, being alone." (James 2:17)

Do I demonstrate my thankfulness to my parents by diligently caring for all that God has given me through their labor and sacrifice?

"Moreover it is required in stewards, that a man be found faithful." (1 Corinthians 4:2)

"…but the substance of a diligent man is precious." (Proverbs 12:27b)

"There is treasure to be desired and oil in the dwelling of the wise; but a foolish man spendeth it up." (Proverbs 21:20)

Am I contributing to an atmosphere of joy in our home?

"But let all those that put their trust in thee rejoice: let them ever shout for joy, because thou defendest them: let them also that love thy name be joyful in thee." (Psalm 5:11)

"A merry heart maketh a cheerful countenance: but by sorrow of the heart the spirit is broken." (Proverbs 15:13)

"If ye know these things, happy are ye if ye do them." (John 13:17)

"My soul shall be satisfied as with marrow and fatness; and my mouth shall praise thee with joyful lips." (Psalm 63:5)

"Rejoice in the Lord alway: and again I say, rejoice." (Philippians 4:4)

Do I in any way imply that my parents are to blame for any of the areas in which I am discontent?

"For from within, out of the heart of men, proceed evil thoughts, adulteries, fornications, murders, thefts, covetousness, wickedness, deceit, lasciviousness, an evil eye, blasphemy, pride, foolishness: all these evil things come from within, and defile the man." (Mark 7:21-23)

"Not that I speak in respect of want: for I have learned, in whatsoever state I am, therewith to be content." (Philippians 4:11)

Do I remember that when I murmur against my parents I am really murmuring against my loving and sovereign Lord?

"Nay but, O man, who art thou that repliest against God? Shall the thing formed say to him that formed it, Why hast thou made me thus?" (Romans 9:20)

"And in the morning, then ye shall see the glory of the LORD; for that he heareth your murmurings against the LORD: and what are we, that ye murmur against us? And Moses said, This shall be, when the LORD shall give you in the evening flesh to eat, and in the morning bread to the full; for that the LORD heareth your murmurings which ye murmur against him: and what are we? Your murmurings are not against us, but against the LORD." (Exodus 16:7-8)

Am I thankful for my parents' strengths, or do I proudly focus on their weaknesses and mistakes?

"Let us therefore follow after the things which make for peace, and things wherewith one may edify another." (Romans 14:19)

"Finally, brethren, whatsoever things are true, whatsoever things are honest, whatsoever things are just, whatsoever things are pure, whatsoever things are lovely, whatsoever things are of good report; if there be any virtue, and if there be any praise, think on these things." (Philippians 4:8)

Do I exercise self-control over my thoughts, not allowing myself to brood over offenses, worry about the future, or indulge in self-pity?

"Take therefore no thought for the morrow: for the morrow shall take thought for the things of itself. Sufficient unto the day is the evil thereof." (Matthew 6:34)

"He that hath no rule over his own spirit is like a city that is broken down, and without walls." (Proverbs 25:28)

"Casting down imaginations, and every high thing that exalteth itself against the knowledge of God, and bringing into captivity every thought to the obedience of Christ." (2 Corinthians 10:5)

Am I thankful for the hardships that sometimes result from my parents' mistakes, knowing that God will use them to help each member of the family grow?

"It is good for me that I have been afflicted; that I might learn thy statutes." (Psalm 119:71)

"If thou faint in the day of adversity, thy strength is small." (Proverbs 24:10)

"Beloved, think it not strange concerning the fiery trial which is to try you, as though some strange thing happened unto you: but rejoice, inasmuch as ye are partakers of Christ's sufferings; that, when his glory shall be revealed, ye may be glad also with exceeding joy." (1 Peter 4:12-13)

Do I trust God to be in control of all circumstances, bringing glory to Himself in the way that He chooses?

"For I know the thoughts that I think toward you, saith the LORD, thoughts of peace, and not of evil, to give you an expected end." (Jeremiah 29:11)

"He staggered not at the promise of God through unbelief; but was strong in faith, giving glory to God; and being fully persuaded that, what he had promised, he was able also to perform." (Romans 4:21)

"Ah Lord GOD! behold, thou hast made the heaven and the earth by thy great power and stretched out arm, and there is nothing too hard for thee." (Jeremiah 32:17)

I honor my parents through:

Imitation of Their Virtues and Graces

My parents, by God's grace, are made in God's image. If they are believers, God is continually maturing them to be more and more conformed to the image of Christ. If they are unbelievers, their lives will still reflect the character of Christ in many ways. I demonstrate my respect for my parents and their God-ordained role in my life by focusing on their virtues and seeking to reproduce those in my own life.

Am I aware of, and am I thankful for, the strengths and godly traits that God in His mercy has granted my parents?

"Finally, brethren, whatsoever things are true, whatsoever things are honest, whatsoever things are just, whatsoever things are pure, whatsoever things are lovely, whatsoever things are of good report; if there be any virtue, and if there be any praise, think on these things." (Philippians 4:8)

Do I admire and respect my parents, or am I embarrassed by or ashamed of them?

"Children's children are the crown of old men; and the glory of children are their fathers." (Proverbs 17:6)

Do I seek to imitate my parents' strengths? Do I thank God for, and seek to imitate, the reflections of Christ's character evident in their lives?

"My son, give me thine heart, and let thine eyes observe my ways." (Proverbs 23:26)

"Brethren, be followers together of me, and mark them which walk so as ye have us for an ensample." (Philippians 3:17)

"Remember them which have the rule over you, who have spoken unto you the word of God: whose faith follow, considering the end of their conversation." (Hebrews 13:7)

Am I willing to be instructed by my parents?

"Hear thou, my son, and be wise, and guide thine heart in the way." (Proverbs 23:19)

"Apply thine heart unto instruction, and thine ears to the words of knowledge." (Proverbs 23:12)

"Hear, ye children, the instruction of a father, and attend to know understanding. For I give you good doctrine, forsake ye not my law. For I was my father's son, tender and only beloved in the sight of my mother. He taught me also, and said unto me, let thine heart retain my words: keep my commandments, and live. Get wisdom, get understanding: forget it not; neither decline from the words of my mouth." (Proverbs 4:1-5)

Do I seek to mature in areas where I am weak and my parents are strong, learning from their example and instruction?

"The just man walketh in his integrity: his children are blessed after him." (Proverbs 20:7)

"I have taught thee in the way of wisdom; I have led thee in right paths. When thou goest, thy steps shall not be straitened; and when thou runnest, thou shalt not stumble." (Proverbs 4:11-12)

Do I rebel against the godly practices and convictions of my parents, or do I see them as a God-given blessing and opportunity for me to grow in my areas of weakness?

"That ye might walk worthy of the Lord unto all pleasing, being fruitful in every good work, and increasing in the knowledge of God." (Colossians 1:10)

"That ye be not slothful, but followers of them who through faith and patience inherit the promises." (Hebrews 6:12)

Do I encourage and follow my parents in godliness, or do I resist them and tempt them to abandon what they know is right?

"And let us consider one another to provoke unto love and to good works." (Hebrews 10:24)

"Whoso causeth the righteous to go astray in an evil way, he shall fall himself into his own pit: but the upright shall have good things in possession." (Proverbs 28:10)

Do I attempt to use my parents' failures and shortcomings as an excuse to ignore their godly instruction and example?

"See that none render evil for evil unto any man; but ever follow that which is good, both among yourselves, and to all men." (1 Thessalonians 5:15)

Do I seek God's wisdom and strength to not follow my parents' example in areas of sin or rebellion?

"But thou, O man of God, flee these things; and follow after righteousness, godliness, faith, love, patience, meekness." (1 Timothy 6:11)

"Flee also youthful lusts: but follow righteousness, faith, charity, peace, with them that call on the Lord out of a pure heart." (2 Timothy 2:22)

"That the generation to come might know them, even the children which should be born; who should arise and declare them to their children: that they might set their hope in God, and not forget the works of God, but keep his commandments: and might not be as their fathers, a stubborn and rebellious generation; a generation that set not their heart aright, and whose spirit was not steadfast with God." (Psalm 78:6-8)

I honor my parents with:

Willing Obedience to Their Lawful Commands

A true and godly fear of my parents will include a sincere desire and willingness to obey them. I will trust them because they are acting as God's representatives in my life. I will want to please them with my attitudes and actions because I respect them. Only when they ask me to disobey God's higher authority will I consider going against their commands.

Am I obeying God by obeying my parents, His delegated authorities over me?

"Children, obey your parents in all things: for this is well pleasing unto the Lord." (Colossians 3:20)

"Let every soul be subject unto the higher powers. For there is no power but of God: the powers that be are ordained of God." (Romans 13:1)

"Giving thanks always for all things unto God and the Father in the name of our Lord Jesus Christ; submitting yourselves one to another in the fear of God." (Ephesians 5:20-21)

Am I humbly resting under the authority of my parents, acknowledging their right to rule over me?

"Children, obey your parents in the Lord: for this is right. Honour thy father and mother; (which is the first commandment with promise;) that it may be well with thee, and thou mayest live long on the earth. And, ye fathers, provoke not your children to wrath: but bring them up in the nurture and admonition of the Lord." (Ephesians 6:1-4)

"Obey them that have the rule over you, and submit yourselves: for they watch for your souls, as they that must give account, that they may do it with joy, and not with grief: for that is unprofitable for you." (Hebrews 13:17)

Do I believe that God will sovereignly direct my life through my parents?

"My son, keep thy father's commandment, and forsake not the law of thy mother: bind them continually upon thine heart, and tie them about thy neck. When thou goest, it shall lead thee; when thou sleepest, it shall keep thee; and when thou awakest, it shall talk with thee. For the commandment is a lamp; and the law is light; and reproofs of instruction are the way of life." (Proverbs 6:20-23)

"Submit yourselves to every ordinance of man for the Lord's sake: whether it be to the king, as supreme; or unto governors, as unto them that are sent by him for the punishment of evildoers, and for the praise of them that do well." (1 Peter 2:13-14)

Do I remember and believe that God will bless me as I obey my parents?

"My son, forget not my law; but let thine heart keep my commandments: for length of days, and long life, and peace, shall they add to thee." (Proverbs 3:1-2)

"Honour thy father and thy mother: that thy days may be long upon the land which the LORD thy God giveth thee." (Exodus 20:12)

Am I thankful for the authority my parents exercise over me?

"Train up a child in the way he should go: and when he is old, he will not depart from it." (Proverbs 22:6)

"Obey them that have the rule over you, and submit yourselves: for they watch for your souls, as they that must give account..." (Hebrews 13:17a)

"And we beseech you, brethren, to know them which labour among you, and are over you in the Lord, and admonish you; and to esteem them very highly in love for their work's sake. And be at peace among yourselves." (1 Thessalonians 5:12-13)

"It is good for a man that he bear the yoke in his youth." (Lamentations 3:27)

Do I pray each day for a submissive heart and the strength to trust and obey God and my parents?

"Faithful is he that calleth you, who also will do it." (1 Thessalonians 5:24)

"And he said unto me, My grace is sufficient for thee: for my strength is made perfect in weakness. Most gladly therefore will I rather glory in my infirmities, that the power of Christ may rest upon me." (2 Corinthians 12:9)

"For Ezra had prepared his heart to seek the law of the LORD, and to do it . . ." (Ezra 7:10a)

Do I honor and obey my parents' instructions wholeheartedly and without resisting, arguing, grumbling, or pouting?

"Only by pride cometh contention: but with the well advised is wisdom." (Proverbs 13:10)

"Servants, obey in all things your masters according to the flesh; not with eyeservice, as menpleasers; but in singleness of heart, fearing God: and whatsoever ye do, do it heartily, as to the Lord, and not unto men." (Colossians 3:22-23)

"Whatsoever thy hand findeth to do, do it with thy might; for there is no work, nor device, nor knowledge, nor wisdom, in the grave, whither thou goest." (Ecclesiastes 9:10)

"Do all things without murmurings and disputings." (Philippians 2:14)

Do I obey immediately?

"I made haste, and delayed not to keep thy commandments." (Psalm 119:60)

Do I humbly submit my will to the will of my parents?

"No man can serve two masters: for either he will hate the one, and love the other; or else he will hold to the one, and despise the other. Ye cannot serve God and mammon." (Matthew 6:24)

"A double minded man is unstable in all his ways." (James 1:8)

Do I seek to surrender my will to my parents in the same way that Jesus submitted to His Father's will?

"And he was withdrawn from them about a stone's cast, and kneeled down, and prayed, saying, Father, if thou be willing, remove this cup from me: nevertheless not my will, but thine, be done." (Luke 22:41-42)

"Jesus saith unto them, My meat is to do the will of him that sent me, and to finish his work." (John 4:34)

"For I came down from heaven, not to do mine own will, but the will of him that sent me." (John 6:38)

Do I set an example before my siblings of proper submission to the authority of my parents? Would they consider me an obedient and respectful son or daughter?

"Those things, which ye have both learned, and received, and heard, and seen in me, do: and the God of peace shall be with you." (Philippians 4:9)

Do I listen carefully to what my parents say so that I will be able to carry out their instructions accurately?

"Therefore all things whatsoever ye would that men should do to you, do ye even so to them: for this is the law and the prophets." (Matthew 7:12)

"Wherefore, my beloved brethren, let every man be swift to hear, slow to speak, slow to wrath." (James 1:19)

"As the cold of snow in the time of harvest, so is a faithful messenger to them that send him: for he refresheth the soul of his masters." (Proverbs 25:13)

Can my parents trust me to faithfully fulfill a responsibility that they assign to me?

"Moreover it is required in stewards, that a man be found faithful." (1 Corinthians 4:2)

"Confidence in an unfaithful man in time of trouble is like a broken tooth, and a foot out of joint." (Proverbs 25:19)

"He also that is slothful in his work is brother to him that is a great waster." (Proverbs 18:9)

"He that is faithful in that which is least is faithful also in much: and he that is unjust in the least is unjust also in much." (Luke 16:10)

Do I accept my parents' decisions and follow their leadership with a willing and cheerful attitude, even when I disagree with them?

"Be not wise in thine own eyes: fear the LORD, and depart from evil. It shall be health to thy navel, and marrow to thy bones." (Proverbs 3:7-8)

"Every way of a man is right in his own eyes: but the LORD pondereth the hearts." (Proverbs 21:2)

"And if a kingdom be divided against itself, that kingdom cannot stand. And if a house be divided against itself, that house cannot stand." (Mark 3:24-25)

Do I honor and obey my parents' stated convictions and instructions, even when I am not with them?

"The eyes of the LORD are in every place, beholding the evil and the good." (Proverbs 15:3)

"Servants, obey in all things your masters according to the flesh; not with eyeservice, as menpleasers; but in singleness of heart, fearing God: and whatsoever ye do, do it heartily, as to the Lord, and not unto men; knowing that of the Lord ye shall receive the reward of the inheritance: for ye serve the Lord Christ." (Colossians 3:22-24)

"Wherefore, my beloved, as ye have always obeyed, not as in my presence only, but now much more in my absence, work out your own salvation with fear and trembling." (Philippians 2:12)

Do I follow my parents' stated convictions and instructions, even when they may not be faithful to them themselves? Do I do what they lawfully want me to do regardless of their own actions?

"And who is he that will harm you, if ye be followers of that which is good?" (1 Peter 3:13)

"And above all things have fervent charity among yourselves: for charity shall cover the multitude of sins." (1 Peter 4:8)

Do I refuse to challenge or ignore the authority of my parents because I fear God and the promised results of disobeying Him?

"It is a fearful thing to fall into the hands of the living God." (Hebrews 10:31)

"And Samuel said, Hath the LORD as great delight in burnt offerings and sacrifices, as in obeying the voice of the LORD? Behold, to obey is better than sacrifice, and to hearken than the fat of rams. For rebellion is as the sin of witchcraft, and stubbornness is as iniquity and idolatry. Because thou hast rejected the word of the LORD, he hath also rejected thee from being king." (1 Samuel 15:22-23)

Do I confess my sin and ask forgiveness of God and my parents when I have not been submissive to them?

"For I will declare mine iniquity; I will be sorry for my sin." (Psalm 38:18)

"He that covereth his sins shall not prosper: but whoso confesseth and forsaketh them shall have mercy." (Proverbs 28:13)

"If we confess our sins, he is faithful and just to forgive us our sins, and to cleanse us from all unrighteousness. If we say that we have not sinned, we make him a liar, and his word is not in us." (1 John 1:9-10)

After confessing my disobedience and asking forgiveness, do I demonstrate my repentance by making restitution, fulfilling what is required of me, and seeking to promote peace and joy in the relationship?

"I thought on my ways, and turned my feet unto thy testimonies." (Psalm 119:59)

"Now I rejoice, not that ye were made sorry, but that ye sorrowed to repentance: for ye were made sorry after a godly manner, that ye might receive damage by us in nothing." (2 Corinthians 7:9)

"Bring forth therefore fruits meet for repentance." (Matthew 3:8)

"Depart from evil, and do good; seek peace, and pursue it." (Psalm 34:14)

When obedience to my parents would require me to clearly sin, do I, with prayer, humility, and respect, claim God and His Word as my final authority?

"Then Peter and the other apostles answered and said, We ought to obey God rather than men." (Acts 5:29)

"Rebuke not an elder, but entreat him as a father; and the younger men as brethren." (1 Timothy 5:1)

After I have respectfully appealed to my parents when they have commanded me to sin, have I sought the counsel and protection of the authorities in my church?

"Moreover if thy brother shall trespass against thee, go and tell him his fault between thee and him alone: if he shall hear thee, thou hast gained thy brother. But if he will not hear thee, then take with thee one or two more, that in the mouth of two or three witnesses every word may be established. And if he shall neglect to hear them, tell it unto the church: but if he neglect to hear the church, let him be unto thee as an heathen man and a publican." (Matthew 18:15-17)

I honor my parents with:

Willing Obedience to Their Lawful Counsels

Honoring my parents will include honoring their opinions and counsel. God has appointed them as His representative authorities in my life, and He will lead me through their guidance and advice. I should recognize my parents as my primary source of counsel, actively seeking their guidance, and governing my actions according to their instruction. I must thankfully and humbly welcome the counsel they offer, not resenting their opinions and guidance.

Am I willing to listen to and consider opinions that differ from my own?

"He that answereth a matter before he heareth it, it is folly and shame unto him." (Proverbs 18:13)

"Without counsel purposes are disappointed: but in the multitude of counsellers they are established." (Proverbs 15:22)

"Where no counsel is, the people fall: but in the multitude of counsellers there is safety." (Proverbs 11:14)

"Wherefore, my beloved brethren, let every man be swift to hear, slow to speak, slow to wrath: for the wrath of man worketh not the righteousness of God." (James 1:19-20)

"The heart of the prudent getteth knowledge; and the ear of the wise seeketh knowledge." (Proverbs 18:15)

Am I willing to accept counsel? Am I teachable?

"Give instruction to a wise man, and he will be yet wiser: teach a just man, and he will increase in learning." (Proverbs 9:9)

"Trust in the LORD with all thine heart; and lean not unto thine own understanding. In all thy ways acknowledge him, and he shall direct thy paths." (Proverbs 3:5-6)

"I will instruct thee and teach thee in the way which thou shalt go: I will guide thee with mine eye. Be ye not as the horse, or as the mule, which have no understanding: whose mouth must be held in with bit and bridle, lest they come near unto thee." (Psalm 32:8-9)

Do I pray for God's help in submitting myself to the counsel of my parents?

"But he giveth more grace. Wherefore he saith, God resisteth the proud, but giveth grace unto the humble. Submit yourselves therefore to God. Resist the devil, and he will flee from you." (James 4:6-7)

"Likewise, ye younger, submit yourselves unto the elder. Yea, all of you be subject one to another, and be clothed with humility: for God resisteth the proud, and giveth grace to the humble." (1 Peter 5:5)

Do I trust God to direct me through the guidance and instruction of my parents?

"Hear thou, my son, and be wise, and guide thine heart in the way." (Proverbs 23:19)

"There are many devices in a man's heart; nevertheless the counsel of the LORD, that shall stand." (Proverbs 19:21)

Do I believe that my parents are wiser than I am?

"He that trusteth in his own heart is a fool: but whoso walketh wisely, he shall be delivered." (Proverbs 28:26)

"Be not wise in thine own eyes: fear the LORD, and depart from evil. It shall be health to thy navel, and marrow to thy bones." (Proverbs 3:7-8)

"The way of a fool is right in his own eyes: but he that hearkeneth unto counsel is wise." (Proverbs 12:15)

Do I give proper weight and value to my parents' opinions and insights?

"Ointment and perfume rejoice the heart: so doth the sweetness of a man's friend by hearty counsel." (Proverbs 27:9)

"A word fitly spoken is like apples of gold in pictures of silver." (Proverbs 25:11)

"Receive my instruction, and not silver; and knowledge rather than choice gold. For wisdom is better than rubies; and all the things that may be desired are not to be compared to it." (Proverbs 8:10-11)

"There is gold, and a multitude of rubies: but the lips of knowledge are a precious jewel." (Proverbs 20:15)

Am I thankful for the wisdom that I can gain from my parents' experience, insights, maturity, and understanding of me?

"Now no chastening for the present seemeth to be joyous, but grievous: nevertheless afterward it yieldeth the peaceable fruit of righteousness unto them which are exercised thereby. Wherefore lift up the hands which hang down, and the feeble knees; and make straight paths for your feet, lest that which is lame be turned out of the way; but let it rather be healed." (Hebrews 12:11-13)

"Iron sharpeneth iron; so a man sharpeneth the countenance of his friend." (Proverbs 27:17)

"My son, hear the instruction of thy father, and forsake not the law of thy mother: for they shall be an ornament of grace unto thy head, and chains about thy neck." (Proverbs 1:8-9)

Do I seek and value my parents' insights and wisdom regarding spiritual matters, decisions, friendships, and other matters of life?

"Remember them which have the rule over you, who have spoken unto you the word of God: whose faith follow, considering the end of their conversation." (Hebrews 13:7)

"Hear counsel, and receive instruction, that thou mayest be wise in thy latter end." (Proverbs 19:20)

"Without counsel purposes are disappointed: but in the multitude of counsellors they are established." (Proverbs 15:22)

"The heart of the prudent getteth knowledge; and the ear of the wise seeketh knowledge." (Proverbs 18:15)

"Counsel in the heart of man is like deep water; but a man of understanding will draw it out." (Proverbs 20:5)

"Every purpose is established by counsel: and with good advice make war." (Proverbs 20:18)

Am I thankful for my parents' counsel and guidance?

"He that rebuketh a man afterwards shall find more favour than he that flattereth with the tongue." (Proverbs 28:23)

"And these words, which I command thee this day, shall be in thine heart: and thou shalt teach them diligently unto thy children, and shalt talk of them when thou sittest in thine house, and when thou walkest by the way, and when thou liest down, and when thou risest up." (Deuteronomy 6:6-7)

Do I follow the advice of my parents?

"For if any be a hearer of the word, and not a doer, he is like unto a man beholding his natural face in a glass: for he beholdeth himself, and goeth his way, and straightway forgetteth what manner of man he was. But whoso looketh into the perfect law of liberty, and continueth therein, he being not a forgetful hearer, but a doer of the work, this man shall be blessed in his deed." (James 1:23-25)

"Seest thou a man wise in his own conceit? there is more hope of a fool than of him." (Proverbs 26:12)

"The way of a fool is right in his own eyes: but he that hearkeneth unto counsel is wise." (Proverbs 12:15)

"As an earring of gold, and an ornament of fine gold, so is a wise reprover upon an obedient ear." (Proverbs 25:12)

Do I recognize that God will bless me as I accept the counsel and direction of my parents?

"My son, hear the instruction of thy father, and forsake not the law of thy mother: for they shall be an ornament of grace unto thy head, and chains about thy neck." (Proverbs 1:8-9)

"He that getteth wisdom loveth his own soul: he that keepeth understanding shall find good." (Proverbs 19:8)

"My son, attend to my words; incline thine ear unto my sayings. Let them not depart from thine eyes; keep them in the midst of thine heart. For they are life unto those that find them, and health to all their flesh." (Proverbs 4:20-22)

"What man is he that feareth the LORD? him shall he teach in the way that he shall choose." (Psalm 25:12)

Do I pray, asking God to direct my parents' thoughts and counsel according to His will?

"The king's heart is in the hand of the LORD, as the rivers of water: he turneth it whithersoever he will." (Proverbs 21:1)

"The preparations of the heart in man, and the answer of the tongue, is from the LORD." (Proverbs 16:1)

Do I seek to always do what I know my parents would lawfully want me to do?

"Therefore to him that knoweth to do good, and doeth it not, to him it is sin." (James 4:17)

"Not with eyeservice, as menpleasers; but as the servants of Christ, doing the will of God from the heart." (Ephesians 6:6)

Do I value the opinions of my parents more than the opinions of my friends?

"He that walketh with wise men shall be wise: but a companion of fools shall be destroyed." (Proverbs 13:20)

"Blessed is the man that walketh not in the counsel of the ungodly, nor standeth in the way of sinners, nor sitteth in the seat of the scornful. But his delight is in the law of the LORD; and in his law doth he meditate day and night. And he shall be like a tree planted by the rivers of water, that bringeth forth his fruit in his season; his leaf also shall not wither; and whatsoever he doeth shall prosper." (Psalm 1:1-3)

"It is better to hear the rebuke of the wise, than for a man to hear the song of fools." (Ecclesiastes 7:5)

Do I humbly entreat my parents when I believe their counsel is contrary to God's Word?

"Likewise, ye younger, submit yourselves unto the elder. Yea, all of you be subject one to another, and be clothed with humility: for God resisteth the proud, and giveth grace to the humble." (1 Peter 5:5)

"Rebuke not an elder, but entreat him as a father; and the younger men as brethren." (1 Timothy 5:1)

"Brethren, if a man be overtaken in a fault, ye which are spiritual, restore such an one in the spirit of meekness; considering thyself, lest thou also be tempted." (Galatians 6:1)

"A soft answer turneth away wrath: but grievous words stir up anger." (Proverbs 15:1)

I honor my parents by giving:
Due Submission to Their Corrections

God has placed me under the authority of my parents, and He commands my obedience to them. My parents' faithful corrections and discipline, combined with my humble submission, will be used by God to make me more like His Son Jesus. When I gratefully acknowledge my position under my parents, I will humbly yield to their discipline, thankful for their faithful ministry that steers me away from error and onto the path of obedience.

Do I recognize that God has given my parents the responsibility to guard and lead me spiritually and to help me recognize and repent of sin in my life?

"Obey them that have the rule over you, and submit yourselves: for they watch for your souls, as they that must give account, that they may do it with joy, and not with grief: for that is unprofitable for you." (Hebrews 13:17)

"But exhort one another daily, while it is called today; lest any of you be hardened through the deceitfulness of sin." (Hebrews 3:13)

"Train up a child in the way he should go: and when he is old, he will not depart from it." (Proverbs 22:6)

Do I recognize that my parents are doing what God requires of them when they correct and discipline me?

"Withhold not correction from the child: for if thou beatest him with the rod, he shall not die. Thou shalt beat him with the rod, and shalt deliver his soul from hell." (Proverbs 23:13-14)

"The rod and reproof give wisdom: but a child left to himself bringeth his mother to shame." (Proverbs 29:15)

"And thou shalt teach them diligently unto thy children, and shalt talk of them when thou sittest in thine house, and when thou walkest by the way, and when thou liest down, and when thou risest up." (Deuteronomy 6:7)

Do I recognize that God will correct me and guide me through the correction and guidance of my parents?

"Foolishness is bound in the heart of a child; but the rod of correction shall drive it far from him." (Proverbs 22:15)

"My son, despise not the chastening of the LORD; neither be weary of his correction: for whom the LORD loveth he correcteth; even as a father the son in whom he delighteth." (Proverbs 3:11-12)

Do I thank God for the love my parents are expressing for me as they choose to correct and discipline me?

"Faithful are the wounds of a friend; but the kisses of an enemy are deceitful." (Proverbs 27:6)

"Now no chastening for the present seemeth to be joyous, but grievous: nevertheless afterward it yieldeth the peaceable fruit of righteousness unto them which are exercised thereby." (Hebrews 12:11)

"Let the righteous smite me; it shall be a kindness: and let him reprove me; it shall be an excellent oil, which shall not break my head: for yet my prayer also shall be in their calamities." (Psalm 141:5)

Do I express gratitude to my parents when they confront me about sin in my life?

"That he might sanctify and cleanse it with the washing of water by the word, that he might present it to himself a glorious church, not having spot, or wrinkle, or any such thing; but that it should be holy and without blemish." (Ephesians 5:26-27)

"Let the righteous smite me; it shall be a kindness: and let him reprove me; it shall be an excellent oil, which shall not break my head: for yet my prayer also shall be in their calamities." (Psalm 141:5)

"If ye endure chastening, God dealeth with you as with sons; for what son is he whom the father chasteneth not? But if ye be without chastisement, whereof all are partakers, then are ye bastards, and not sons. Furthermore we have

had fathers of our flesh which corrected us, and we gave them reverence: shall we not much rather be in subjection unto the Father of spirits, and live? For they verily for a few days chastened us after their own pleasure; but he for our profit, that we might be partakers of his holiness." (Hebrews 12:7-10)

Do I respond with love and humility when confronted with my faults and sins, listening carefully rather than arguing or defending myself?

"A wise son heareth his father's instruction: but a scorner heareth not rebuke." (Proverbs 13:1)

"The ear that heareth the reproof of life abideth among the wise. He that refuseth instruction despiseth his own soul: but he that heareth reproof getteth understanding." (Proverbs 15:31-32)

"Give instruction to a wise man, and he will be yet wiser: teach a just man, and he will increase in learning." (Proverbs 9:9)

Do I humbly accept responsibility for my actions, not making excuses or blaming others for my sins?

"The soul that sinneth, it shall die. The son shall not bear the iniquity of the father, neither shall the father bear the iniquity of the son: the righteousness of the righteous shall be upon him, and the wickedness of the wicked shall be upon him. But if the wicked will turn from all his sins that he hath committed, and keep all my statutes, and do that which is lawful and right, he shall surely live, he shall not die." (Ezekiel 18:20-21)

Am I willing to admit when I am wrong?

"He that covereth his sins shall not prosper: but whoso confesseth and forsaketh them shall have mercy." (Proverbs 28:13)

"Humble yourselves in the sight of the Lord, and he shall lift you up." (James 4:10)

"If we say that we have no sin, we deceive ourselves, and the truth is not in us. If we confess our sins, he is faithful and just to forgive us our sins, and to cleanse us from all unrighteousness." (1 John 1:8-9)

Am I thankful for the pain of correction, knowing that God is using it to make me more like Jesus?

"It is good for me that I have been afflicted; that I might learn thy statutes." (Psalm 119:71)

"If ye endure chastening, God dealeth with you as with sons; for what son is he whom the father chasteneth not? But if ye be without chastisement, whereof all are partakers, then are ye bastards, and not sons. Furthermore we have had fathers of our flesh which corrected us, and we gave them reverence: shall we not much rather be in subjection unto the Father of spirits, and live? For they verily for a few days chastened us after their own pleasure; but he for our profit, that we might be partakers of his holiness. Now no chastening for the present seemeth to be joyous, but

grievous: nevertheless afterward it yieldeth the peaceable fruit of righteousness unto them which are exercised thereby." (Hebrews 12:7-11)

"Faithful are the wounds of a friend; but the kisses of an enemy are deceitful." (Proverbs 27:6)

When I have been confronted with my sin am I quick to humble myself before God, acknowledging my sin and need of forgiveness?

"Create in me a clean heart, O God; and renew a right spirit within me." (Psalm 51:10)

"For I will declare mine iniquity; I will be sorry for my sin." (Psalm 38:18)

"I acknowledged my sin unto thee, and mine iniquity have I not hid. I said, I will confess my transgressions unto the LORD; and thou forgavest the iniquity of my sin. Selah." (Psalm 32:5)

"Wash me throughly from mine iniquity, and cleanse me from my sin. For I acknowledge my transgressions: and my sin is ever before me. Against thee, thee only, have I sinned, and done this evil in thy sight: that thou mightest be justified when thou speakest, and be clear when thou judgest." (Psalm 51:2-4)

"If we confess our sins, he is faithful and just to forgive us our sins, and to cleanse us from all unrighteousness. If we say that we have not sinned, we make him a liar, and his word is not in us." (1 John 1:9-10)

When I have been confronted with my sin do I confess it and ask forgiveness of those I have offended, and do I make restitution when necessary?

"The sacrifices of God are a broken spirit: a broken and a contrite heart, O God, thou wilt not despise." (Psalm 51:17)

"Confess your faults one to another, and pray one for another, that ye may be healed. The effectual fervent prayer of a righteous man availeth much." (James 5:16)

When my parents confront me with areas of sin in my life, do I demonstrate true repentance by seeking, with God's help, to set aside my sinful habits and to do what is right?

"Depart from evil, and do good; seek peace, and pursue it." (Psalm 34:14)

"Therefore now amend your ways and your doings, and obey the voice of the LORD your God; and the LORD will repent him of the evil that he hath pronounced against you." (Jeremiah 26:13)

"I thought on my ways, and turned my feet unto thy testimonies." (Psalm 119:59)

"A reproof entereth more into a wise man than an hundred stripes into a fool." (Proverbs 17:10)

Do I recognize that God will use my parents' actions and words, even if they are unbelievers or immature Christians, to bring me to greater maturity and conformity to Christ's image?

"...being predestinated according to the purpose of him who worketh all things after the counsel of his own will: that we should be to the praise of his glory, who first trusted in Christ." (Ephesians 1:11b-12)

"And we know that all things work together for good to them that love God, to them who are the called according to his purpose. For whom he did foreknow, he also did predestinate to be conformed to the image of his Son, that he might be the firstborn among many brethren." (Romans 8:28-29)

Do I observe and learn from the mistakes and discipline of my siblings?

"Smite a scorner, and the simple will beware: and reprove one that hath understanding, and he will understand knowledge." (Proverbs 19:25)

"When the scorner is punished, the simple is made wise: and when the wise is instructed, he receiveth knowledge." (Proverbs 21:11)

I honor my parents with:

Fidelity to Their Persons and Authority

A godly respect for my parents will result in faithfulness. I will carefully fulfill my duties and obligations to them. I will desire to please them, and will be loyal to them and their instruction. I will seek to help and encourage them.

Do I trust that God, in His perfect wisdom, has chosen my parents as His delegated authorities over me?

"Let every soul be subject unto the higher powers. For there is no power but of God: the powers that be are ordained of God." (Romans 13:1)

Do I humbly allow my parents to help guard my heart from influences that would draw me away from them and the goals they have set for me and our family?

"My son, give me thine heart, and let thine eyes observe my ways." (Proverbs 23:26)

"Keep thy heart with all diligence; for out of it are the issues of life." (Proverbs 4:23)

Am I a content and cheerful member of my family?

"A merry heart maketh a cheerful countenance: but by sorrow of the heart the spirit is broken." (Proverbs 15:13)

"All the days of the afflicted are evil: but he that is of a merry heart hath a continual feast." (Proverbs 15:15)

"A merry heart doeth good like a medicine: but a broken spirit drieth the bones." (Proverbs 17:22)

"But godliness with contentment is great gain." (1 Timothy 6:6)

Do I loyally support and encourage my parents in their leadership and decisions?

"A friend loveth at all times, and a brother is born for adversity." (Proverbs 17:17)

"Heaviness in the heart of man maketh it stoop: but a good word maketh it glad." (Proverbs 12:25)

"[Charity] beareth all things, believeth all things, hopeth all things, endureth all things." (1 Corinthians 13:7)

Am I enthusiastically pursuing the goals of our family?

"I therefore, the prisoner of the Lord, beseech you that ye walk worthy of the vocation wherewith ye are called, with all lowliness and meekness, with longsuffering, forbearing one another in love; endeavouring to keep the unity of the Spirit in the bond of peace." (Ephesians 4:1-3)

"Behold, how good and how pleasant it is for brethren to dwell together in unity! It is like the precious ointment upon the head, that ran down upon the beard, even Aaron's beard: that went down to the skirts of his garments." (Psalm 133:1-2)

". . . for whither thou goest, I will go; and where thou lodgest, I will lodge: thy people shall be my people, and thy God my God." (Ruth 1:16b)

Do I sincerely desire to please God and my parents in all I do?

"My son, if thine heart be wise, my heart shall rejoice, even mine." (Proverbs 23:15)

"Withhold not good from them to whom it is due, when it is in the power of thine hand to do it." (Proverbs 3:27)

"Let us hear the conclusion of the whole matter: fear God, and keep his commandments: for this is the whole duty of man. For God shall bring every work into judgment, with every secret thing, whether it be good, or whether it be evil." (Ecclesiastes 12:13-14)

"Furthermore then we beseech you, brethren, and exhort you by the Lord Jesus, that as ye have received of us how ye ought to walk and to please God, so ye would abound more and more. For ye know what commandments we gave you by the Lord Jesus." (1 Thessalonians 4:1-2)

Do I lead and encourage my siblings in respectfully following and obeying our parents?

"I will behave myself wisely in a perfect way. O when wilt thou come unto me? I will walk within my house with a perfect heart." (Psalm 101:2)

"Let no man despise thy youth; but be thou an example of the believers, in word, in conversation, in charity, in spirit, in faith, in purity." (1 Timothy 4:12)

"In all things shewing thyself a pattern of good works: in doctrine shewing uncorruptness, gravity, sincerity, sound speech, that cannot be condemned; that he that is of the contrary part may be ashamed, having no evil thing to say of you." (Titus 2:7-8)

Do I continually seek to demonstrate kindness and respect to my parents and siblings?

"As we have therefore opportunity, let us do good unto all men, especially unto them who are of the household of faith." (Galatians 6:10)

"And though I bestow all my goods to feed the poor, and though I give my body to be burned, and have not charity, it profiteth me nothing." (1 Corinthians 13:3)

"My little children, let us not love in word, neither in tongue; but in deed and in truth." (1 John 3:18)

"Be kindly affectioned one to another with brotherly love; in honour preferring one another." (Romans 12:10)

Do I consistently show honor and obedience to my mother, even when my father is not present?

"Not with eyeservice, as menpleasers; but as the servants of Christ, doing the will of God from the heart; with good will doing service, as to the Lord, and not to men: knowing that whatsoever good thing any man doeth, the same shall he receive of the Lord, whether he be bond or free." (Ephesians 6:6-8)

"A wise son maketh a glad father: but a foolish man despiseth his mother." (Proverbs 15:20)

Do I speak respectfully about my parents to others? Do I refrain from criticizing or reviewing their faults with others?

"A good man out of the good treasure of his heart bringeth forth that which is good; and an evil man out of the evil treasure of his heart bringeth forth that which is evil: for of the abundance of the heart his mouth speaketh." (Luke 6:45)

"A froward man soweth strife: and a whisperer separateth chief friends." (Proverbs 16:28)

"He that covereth a transgression seeketh love; but he that repeateth a matter separateth very friends." (Proverbs 17:9)

"But chiefly them that walk after the flesh in the lust of uncleanness, and despise government. Presumptuous are they, selfwilled, they are not afraid to speak evil of dignities." (2 Peter 2:10)

"Likewise also these filthy dreamers defile the flesh, despise dominion, and speak evil of dignities." (Jude 8)

Do I choose to keep company with other children and young people who love and respect their parents?

"He that walketh with wise men shall be wise: but a companion of fools shall be destroyed." (Proverbs 13:20)

"Whoso keepeth the law is a wise son: but he that is a companion of riotous men shameth his father." (Proverbs 28:7)

Do I honor my parents' and family's privacy by not revealing personal, intimate information about them to others?

"As a jewel of gold in a swine's snout, so is a fair woman which is without discretion." (Proverbs 11:22)

"A talebearer revealeth secrets: but he that is of a faithful spirit concealeth the matter." (Proverbs 11:13)

When I have offended and sinned against my parents, do I do all I can to reconcile our relationship?

"A brother offended is harder to be won than a strong city: and their contentions are like the bars of a castle." (Proverbs 18:19)

"If it be possible, as much as lieth in you, live peaceably with all men." (Romans 12:18)

"Be ye angry, and sin not: let not the sun go down upon your wrath." (Ephesians 4:26)

"And herein do I exercise myself, to have always a conscience void of offence toward God, and toward men." (Acts 24:16)

I honor my parents with:

Defense and Maintenance of Their Persons and Authority

I will demonstrate my reverence for God and my parents by actively defending and supporting my parents as they rule over me. Not only must I not question or challenge their right to rule, but I must also defend their leadership against the criticism and attack of others. I will support their decisions, and demonstrate that support to others by cheerfully and quietly obeying my parents in all their lawful commands.

Do I do all I righteously can to support and encourage my parents as they lead, provide, and care for our family?

"And let us consider one another to provoke unto love and to good works." (Hebrews 10:24)

"Let no man seek his own, but every man another's wealth." (1 Corinthians 10:24)

"Wherefore comfort yourselves together, and edify one another, even as also ye do." (1 Thessalonians 5:11)

Am I careful to avoid actions and attitudes that would discourage my father in assuming his role as the head of our family?

"…Knowledge puffeth up, but charity edifieth." (1 Corinthians 8:1b)

"Obey them that have the rule over you, and submit yourselves: for they watch for your souls, as they that must give account, that they may do it with joy, and not with grief: for that is unprofitable for you." (Hebrews 13:17)

"He that gathereth in summer is a wise son: but he that sleepeth in harvest is a son that causeth shame." (Proverbs 10:5)

"A wise son heareth his father's instruction: but a scorner heareth not rebuke." (Proverbs 13:1)

Am I careful to avoid actions and attitudes that would discourage my mother in the service she offers God and our family?

"The proverbs of Solomon. A wise son maketh a glad father: but a foolish son is the heaviness of his mother." (Proverbs 10:1)

"The father of the righteous shall greatly rejoice: and he that begetteth a wise child shall have joy of him. Thy father and thy mother shall be glad, and she that bare thee shall rejoice." (Proverbs 23:24-25)

"A foolish son is a grief to his father, and bitterness to her that bare him." (Proverbs 17:25)

Do I willingly give up my own desires in order to help my parents, assisting them in their daily tasks, offering my strength and energy for their aid?

"We then that are strong ought to bear the infirmities of the weak, and not to please ourselves. Let every one of us please his neighbour for his good to edification." (Romans 15:1-2)

"There is that scattereth, and yet increaseth; and there is that withholdeth more than is meet, but it tendeth to poverty. The liberal soul shall be made fat: and he that watereth shall be watered also himself." (Proverbs 11:24-25)

"The desire of the slothful killeth him; for his hands refuse to labour. He coveteth greedily all the day long: but the righteous giveth and spareth not." (Proverbs 21:25-26)

"Give, and it shall be given unto you; good measure, pressed down, and shaken together, and running over, shall men give into your bosom. For with the same measure that ye mete withal it shall be measured to you again." (Luke 6:38)

Do I, with humble word and example, encourage my siblings to obey our parents?

"Now we exhort you, brethren, warn them that are unruly, comfort the feebleminded, support the weak, be patient toward all men." (1 Thessalonians 5:14)

"Put them in mind to be subject to principalities and powers, to obey magistrates, to be ready to every good work." (Titus 3:1)

"Be ye followers of me, even as I also am of Christ." (1 Corinthians 11:1)

Do I refuse to question or challenge my parents' right to counsel and lead our family?

"Let no corrupt communication proceed out of your mouth, but that which is good to the use of edifying, that it may minister grace unto the hearers." (Ephesians 4:29)

"Can two walk together, except they be agreed?" (Amos 3:3)

"And Jesus knew their thoughts, and said unto them, Every kingdom divided against itself is brought to desolation; and every city or house divided against itself shall not stand." (Matthew 12:25)

"Exhort servants to be obedient unto their own masters, and to please them well in all things; not answering again; not purloining, but shewing all good fidelity; that they may adorn the doctrine of God our Saviour in all things." (Titus 2:9-10)

"Therefore let us pursue the things which make for peace and the things by which one may edify another." (Romans 14:19)

Do I speak sincere words of gratitude, praise, and admiration to my parents? Do I openly praise them to others?

"Pleasant words are as an honeycomb, sweet to the soul, and health to the bones." (Proverbs 16:24)

"And let us consider one another to provoke unto love and to good works." (Hebrews 10:24)

"Let every one of us please his neighbour for his good to edification." (Romans 15:2)

"Give her of the fruit of her hands; and let her own works praise her in the gates." (Proverbs 31:31)

Do my siblings and friends know that I will consistently support my parents' decisions and leadership of the family?

"Behold, how good and how pleasant it is for brethren to dwell together in unity!" (Psalm 133:1)

"Finally, be ye all of one mind, having compassion one of another, love as brethren, be pitiful, be courteous." (1 Peter 3:8)

"No servant can serve two masters: for either he will hate the one, and love the other; or else he will hold to the one, and despise the other. Ye cannot serve God and mammon." (Luke 16:13)

"Be of the same mind one toward another. Mind not high things, but condescend to men of low estate. Be not wise in your own conceits." (Romans 12:16)

"For where envying and strife is, there is confusion and every evil work." (James 3:16)

Do I stand up for my parents and their teaching if my friends criticize or question their judgment?

"My son, fear thou the LORD and the king: and meddle not with them that are given to change: for their calamity shall rise suddenly; and who knoweth the ruin of them both?" (Proverbs 24:21-22)

"Enter not into the path of the wicked, and go not in the way of evil men. Avoid it, pass not by it, turn from it, and pass away." (Proverbs 4:14-15)

"The north wind driveth away rain: so doth an angry countenance a backbiting tongue." (Proverbs 25:23)

"Most men will proclaim every one his own goodness: but a faithful man who can find?" (Proverbs 20:6)

I honor my parents by:

Bearing with Their Infirmities and Covering Them with Love

Because my parents and I are all fallen sinners, our relationship will require love, patience, and forgiveness. My parents, like me, have weaknesses and shortcomings. Like me, they will make mistakes. Like me, they will sin. I must lovingly overlook and refuse to draw attention to their errors and faults. I must remember my own faults and be thankful for the forbearance my parents and others show me. As Christ forgives me, I must also forgive my parents.

Do I expect perfection from my parents, or am I patient with their faults, remembering that I too am imperfect and have faults of my own that they and many others choose to overlook?

"With all lowliness and meekness, with longsuffering, forbearing one another in love; endeavouring to keep the unity of the Spirit in the bond of peace." (Ephesians 4:2-3)

"Shouldest not thou also have had compassion on thy fellowservant, even as I had pity on thee?" (Matthew 18:33)

"But if ye bite and devour one another, take heed that ye be not consumed one of another." (Galatians 5:15)

"Owe no man any thing, but to love one another: for he that loveth another hath fulfilled the law." (Romans 13:8)

Do I show patience and longsuffering toward my parents and their weaknesses in the same way that God has been patient and loving toward me in my own weakness and sin?

"He hath not dealt with us after our sins; nor rewarded us according to our iniquities. For as the heaven is high above the earth, so great is his mercy toward them that fear him." (Psalm 103:10-11)

"For he knoweth our frame; he remembereth that we are dust." (Psalm 103:14)

"This is my commandment, That ye love one another, as I have loved you." (John 15:12)

"Now the God of patience and consolation grant you to be likeminded one toward another according to Christ Jesus." (Romans 15:5)

"And be ye kind one to another, tenderhearted, forgiving one another, even as God for Christ's sake hath forgiven you." (Ephesians 4:32)

Do I always seek to think the best about my parents and their actions, or do I often mistrust them, questioning their motives and actions?

"Charity suffereth long, and is kind; charity envieth not; charity vaunteth not itself, is not puffed up, doth not behave itself unseemly, seeketh not her own, is not easily provoked, thinketh no evil; rejoiceth not in iniquity, but rejoiceth in the truth; beareth all things, believeth all things, hopeth all things, endureth all things. Charity never faileth: but whether there be prophecies, they shall fail; whether there be tongues, they shall cease; whether there be knowledge, it shall vanish away." (1 Corinthians 13:4-8)

"Flee also youthful lusts: but follow righteousness, faith, charity, peace, with them that call on the Lord out of a pure heart." (2 Timothy 2:22)

"With all lowliness and meekness, with longsuffering, forbearing one another in love." (Ephesians 4:2)

"Obey them that have the rule over you, and submit yourselves: for they watch for your souls, as they that must give account, that they may do it with joy, and not with grief: for that is unprofitable for you." (Hebrews 13:17)

Do I lovingly pray for, support, and encourage my parents as they seek, by God's grace, to be conformed to the image of Christ?

"Two are better than one; because they have a good reward for their labour. For if they fall, the one will lift up his fellow: but woe to him that is alone when he falleth; for he hath not another to help him up." (Ecclesiastes 4:9-10)

"Let us therefore follow after the things which make for peace, and things wherewith one may edify another." (Romans 14:19)

Do I show the love of Christ to my parents when either of them has offended me?

"Finally, be ye all of one mind, having compassion one of another, love as brethren, be pitiful, be courteous: not rendering evil for evil, or railing for railing: but contrariwise blessing; knowing that ye are thereunto called, that ye should inherit a blessing." (1 Peter 3:8-9)

"And walk in love, as Christ also hath loved us, and hath given himself for us an offering and a sacrifice to God for a sweetsmelling savour." (Ephesians 5:2)

"I therefore, the prisoner of the Lord, beseech you that ye walk worthy of the vocation wherewith ye are called, with all lowliness and meekness, with longsuffering, forbearing one another in love." (Ephesians 4:1-2)

When faced with the inevitable tests of being an obedient and faithful son or daughter, do I seek comfort and wisdom from God's Word as it is presented in Scripture and in godly instruction from His Word?

"I thought on my ways, and turned my feet unto thy testimonies." (Psalm 119:59)

"For whatsoever things were written aforetime were written for our learning, that we through patience and comfort of the scriptures might have hope." (Romans 15:4)

"Remember the word unto thy servant, upon which thou hast caused me to hope. This is my comfort in my affliction: for thy word hath quickened me." (Psalm 119:49-50)

"Thy word have I hid in mine heart, that I might not sin against thee. Blessed art thou, O LORD: teach me thy statutes." (Psalm 119:11-12)

Am I, by God's grace, resisting the temptation to appoint myself to be a judge of my parents? Am I willing to overlook faults without comment?

"Hatred stirreth up strifes: but love covereth all sins." (Proverbs 10:12)

"And above all things have fervent charity among yourselves: for charity shall cover the multitude of sins." (1 Peter 4:8)

"The discretion of a man deferreth his anger; and it is his glory to pass over a transgression." (Proverbs 19:11)

"Is it fit to say to a king, Thou art wicked? and to princes, Ye are ungodly?" (Job 34:18)

"But why dost thou judge thy brother? or why dost thou set at nought thy brother? for we shall all stand before the judgment seat of Christ." (Romans 14:10)

Do I refuse to question or disagree with my parents in the presence of others?

"Moreover if thy brother shall trespass against thee, go and tell him his fault between thee and him alone: if he shall hear thee, thou hast gained thy brother." (Matthew 18:15)

"To speak evil of no man, to be no brawlers, but gentle, shewing all meekness unto all men." (Titus 3:2)

"Go not forth hastily to strive, lest thou know not what to do in the end thereof, when thy neighbour hath put thee to shame. Debate thy cause with thy neighbour himself; and discover not a secret to another." (Proverbs 25:8-9)

Do I rest in God's sovereignty, knowing that He will accomplish His eternal will through my parents' weaknesses as well as their strengths?

"And he said unto me, My grace is sufficient for thee: for my strength is made perfect in weakness. Most gladly therefore will I rather glory in my infirmities, that the power of Christ may rest upon me." (2 Corinthians 12:9)

"I have set the LORD always before me: because he is at my right hand, I shall not be moved." (Psalm 16:8)

Do I guard my tongue and emotions when I believe my parents are making a mistake?

"A wrathful man stirreth up strife: but he that is slow to anger appeaseth strife." (Proverbs 15:18)

"Be ye angry, and sin not: let not the sun go down upon your wrath: neither give place to the devil." (Ephesians 4:26-27)

"A soft answer turneth away wrath: but grievous words stir up anger." (Proverbs 15:1)

"As coals are to burning coals, and wood to fire; so is a contentious man to kindle strife." (Proverbs 26:21)

Do I allow my parents to make mistakes without shaming them?

"The words of a wise man's mouth are gracious; but the lips of a fool will swallow up himself." (Ecclesiastes 10:12)

"I know both how to be abased, and I know how to abound: every where and in all things I am instructed both to be full and to be hungry, both to abound and to suffer need. I can do all things through Christ which strengtheneth me." (Philippians 4:12-13)

Do I put my trust in God when my parents err?

"There is no fear in love; but perfect love casteth out fear: because fear hath torment. He that feareth is not made perfect in love." (1 John 4:18)

"And he said unto me, My grace is sufficient for thee: for my strength is made perfect in weakness. Most gladly therefore will I rather glory in my infirmities, that the power of Christ may rest upon me." (2 Corinthians 12:9)

"For we have not an high priest which cannot be touched with the feeling of our infirmities; but was in all points tempted like as we are, yet without sin." (Hebrews 4:15)

"The eternal God is thy refuge, and underneath are the everlasting arms. . ." (Deuteronomy 33:27a)

Am I willing to suffer hardship in order to remain faithful to my parents and the covenant relationship we share?

"But what things were gain to me, those I counted loss for Christ. . .That I may know him, and the power of his resurrection, and the fellowship of his sufferings, being made conformable unto his death." (Philippians 3:7, 10)

"Though he were a Son, yet learned he obedience by the things which he suffered." (Hebrews 5:8)

"Hereby perceive we the love of God, because he laid down his life for us: and we ought to lay down our lives for the brethren." (1 John 3:16)

Do I freely forgive my parents' offenses?

"But if ye forgive not men their trespasses, neither will your Father forgive your trespasses." (Matthew 6:15)

"Take heed to yourselves: if thy brother trespass against thee, rebuke him; and if he repent, forgive him. And if he trespass against thee seven times in a day, and seven times in a day turn again to thee, saying, I repent; thou shalt forgive him." (Luke 17:3-4)

"Put on therefore, as the elect of God, holy and beloved, bowels of mercies, kindness, humbleness of mind, meekness, longsuffering; forbearing one another, and forgiving one another, if any man have a quarrel against any: even as Christ forgave you, so also do ye. And above all these things put on charity, which is the bond of perfectness. And let the peace of God rule in your hearts, to the which also ye are called in one body; and be ye thankful." (Colossians 3:12-15)

"He that covereth a transgression seeketh love; but he that repeateth a matter separateth very friends." (Proverbs 17:9)

Do I respond with godly love, even when one or both of my parents do not show love to me?

"And as ye would that men should do to you, do ye also to them likewise. For if ye love them which love you, what thank have ye? for sinners also love those that love them. And if ye do good to them which do good to you, what thank have ye? for sinners also do even the same. And if ye lend to them of whom ye hope to receive, what thank have ye? for sinners also lend to sinners, to receive as much again. But love ye your enemies, and do good, and lend, hoping for nothing again; and your reward shall be great, and ye shall be the children of the Highest: for he is kind unto the unthankful and to the evil. Be ye therefore merciful, as your Father also is merciful. Judge not, and ye shall not be judged: condemn not, and ye shall not be condemned: forgive, and ye shall be forgiven." (Luke 6:31-37)

"If the spirit of the ruler rise up against thee, leave not thy place; for yielding pacifieth great offences." (Ecclesiastes 10:4)

"See that none render evil for evil unto any man; but ever follow that which is good, both among yourselves, and to all men." (1 Thessalonians 5:15)

"And I will very gladly spend and be spent for you; though the more abundantly I love you, the less I be loved." (2 Corinthians 12:15)

"But I say unto you, That ye resist not evil: but whosoever shall smite thee on thy right cheek, turn to him the other also. And if any man will sue thee at the law, and take away thy coat, let him have thy cloak also. And whosoever shall compel thee to go a mile, go with him twain. Give to him that asketh thee, and from him that would borrow of thee turn not thou away." (Matthew 5:39-42)

Do I place my confidence in God if one or both of my parents choose to ignore, neglect, or abandon their responsibilities as spouse or parent in our family?

"The LORD preserveth the strangers; he relieveth the fatherless and widow: but the way of the wicked he turneth upside down." (Psalm 146:9)

"A father of the fatherless, and a judge of the widows, is God in his holy habitation." (Psalm 68:5)

"Leave thy fatherless children, I will preserve them alive; and let thy widows trust in me." (Jeremiah 49:11)

"...[The Lord] will ever be mindful of his covenant." (Psalm 111:5b)

"Cast thy burden upon the LORD, and he shall sustain thee: he shall never suffer the righteous to be moved." (Psalm 55:22)

"He healeth the broken in heart, and bindeth up their wounds." (Psalm 147:3)

Do I rest in God's ability to change circumstances and people, or do I attempt to force change with my own sinful methods?

"The king's heart is in the hand of the LORD, as the rivers of water: he turneth it whithersoever he will." (Proverbs 21:1)

"When the poor and needy seek water, and there is none, and their tongue faileth for thirst, I the LORD will hear them, I the God of Israel will not forsake them. I will open rivers in high places, and fountains in the midst of the valleys: I will make the wilderness a pool of water, and the dry land springs of water. I will plant in the wilderness the cedar, the shittah tree, and the myrtle, and the oil tree; I will set in the desert the fir tree, and the pine, and the box tree together: that they may see, and know, and consider, and understand together, that the hand of the LORD hath done this, and the Holy One of Israel hath created it." (Isaiah 41:17-20)

"And I will give them one heart, and I will put a new spirit within you; and I will take the stony heart out of their flesh, and will give them an heart of flesh: that they may walk in my statutes, and keep mine ordinances, and do them: and they shall be my people, and I will be their God." (Ezekiel 11:19-20)

If I feel that my parents' leadership is not glorifying to God, am I being careful to bring glory to God through my godly response to them?

"Rest in the LORD, and wait patiently for him: fret not thyself because of him who prospereth in his way, because of the man who bringeth wicked devices to pass. Cease from anger, and forsake wrath: fret not thyself in any wise to do evil." (Psalm 37:7-8)

"Whether therefore ye eat, or drink, or whatsoever ye do, do all to the glory of God." (1 Corinthians 10:31)

Do I, with love, respectfully and humbly appeal to my parents when they are in serious sin?

"Brethren, if a man be overtaken in a fault, ye which are spiritual, restore such an one in the spirit of meekness; considering thyself, lest thou also be tempted." (Galatians 6:1)

"Moreover if thy brother shall trespass against thee, go and tell him his fault between thee and him alone: if he shall hear thee, thou hast gained thy brother." (Matthew 18:15)

"Rebuke not an elder, but entreat him as a father; and the younger men as brethren." (1 Timothy 5:1)

In matters of serious sin and neglect, if my parents have not repented after my humble appeals, have I prayerfully brought the matter to the attention of the church leaders? Am I seeking godly counsel and protection?

"But if he will not hear thee, then take with thee one or two more, that in the mouth of two or three witnesses every word may be established. And if he shall neglect to hear them, tell it unto the church: but if he neglect to hear the church, let him be unto thee as a heathen man and a publican." (Matthew 18:16-17)

"Dare any of you, having a matter against another, go to law before the unjust, and not before the saints?" (1 Corinthians 6:1)

"Let all things be done decently and in order." (1 Corinthians 14:40)

"The LORD also will be a refuge for the oppressed, a refuge in times of trouble." (Psalm 9:9)

I honor my parents by being:

An Honor to Them and Their Government

My chief purpose in life is to bring glory to God. In my youth, I will primarily glorify God by honoring and respecting my parents. My life should increase the respect of others for God and my parents as I live a life of obedience and contentment, adorning the teaching of Scripture and the instruction of my parents.

Am I a contented member of my family?

"Not that I speak in respect of want: for I have learned, in whatsoever state I am, therewith to be content." (Philippians 4:11)

"The backslider in heart shall be filled with his own ways: and a good man shall be satisfied from himself." (Proverbs 14:14)

"And having food and raiment let us be therewith content." (1 Timothy 6:8)

Are my attitudes and actions ones of which my parents can be proud?

"Many daughters have done virtuously, but thou excellest them all." (Proverbs 31:29)

"But the fruit of the Spirit is love, joy, peace, longsuffering, gentleness, goodness, faith, meekness, temperance: against such there is no law." (Galatians 5:22-23)

"The father of the righteous shall greatly rejoice: and he that begetteth a wise child shall have joy of him. Thy father and thy mother shall be glad, and she that bare thee shall rejoice." (Proverbs 23:24-25)

Do my attitudes and actions lead others to an increased respect for my parents?

"Submit yourselves to every ordinance of man for the Lord's sake: whether it be to the king, as supreme; or unto governors, as unto them that are sent by him for the punishment of evildoers, and for the praise of them that do well. For so is the will of God, that with well doing ye may put to silence the ignorance of foolish men." (1 Peter 2:13-15)

"As arrows are in the hand of a mighty man; so are children of the youth. Happy is the man that hath his quiver full of them: they shall not be ashamed, but they shall speak with the enemies in the gate." (Psalm 127:4-5)

"By the blessing of the upright the city is exalted: but it is overthrown by the mouth of the wicked." (Proverbs 11:11)

"Dead flies cause the ointment of the apothecary to send forth a stinking savour: so doth a little folly him that is in reputation for wisdom and honour." (Ecclesiastes 10:1)

Am I furthering the goals and ministries of my parents and family?

"And he that sent me is with me: the Father hath not left me alone; for I do always those things that please him." (John 8:29)

"Jesus saith unto them, My meat is to do the will of him that sent me, and to finish his work." (John 4:34)

"So likewise ye, when ye shall have done all those things which are commanded you, say, We are unprofitable servants: we have done that which was our duty to do." (Luke 17:10)

Am I an "example of the believers," growing in obedience and godliness now in my youth?

"Let no man despise thy youth; but be thou an example of the believers, in word, in conversation, in charity, in spirit, in faith, in purity." (1 Timothy 4:12)

"So teach us to number our days, that we may apply our hearts unto wisdom." (Psalm 90:12)

"For thou art my hope, O Lord GOD: thou art my trust from my youth." (Psalm 71:5)

"O God, thou hast taught me from my youth: and hitherto have I declared thy wondrous works." (Psalm 71:17)

"Remember now thy Creator in the days of thy youth, while the evil days come not, nor the years draw nigh, when thou shalt say, I have no pleasure in them." (Ecclesiastes 12:1)

As a daughter, am I seeking to serve God and bring honor to my parents by doing those things that Scripture outlines as good works for women?

"In like manner also, that women adorn themselves in modest apparel, with shamefacedness and sobriety; not with broided hair, or gold, or pearls, or costly array; but (which becometh women professing godliness) with good works." (1 Timothy 2:9-10)

"Who can find a virtuous woman? for her price is far above rubies." (Proverbs 31:10)

"She openeth her mouth with wisdom; and in her tongue is the law of kindness. She looketh well to the ways of her household, and eateth not the bread of idleness. Her children arise up, and call her blessed; her husband also, and he praiseth her. Many daughters have done virtuously, but thou excellest them all. Favour is deceitful, and beauty is vain: but a woman that feareth the LORD, she shall be praised. Give her of the fruit of her hands; and let her own works praise her in the gates." (Proverbs 31:26-31)

"Well reported of for good works; if she have brought up children, if she have lodged strangers, if she have washed the saints' feet, if she have relieved the afflicted, if she have diligently followed every good work."   *(1 Timothy 5:10)*

"That they may teach the young women to be sober, to love their husbands, to love their children, to be discreet, chaste, keepers at home, good, obedient to their own husbands, that the word of God be not blasphemed." *(Titus 2:4-5)*

As a son, am I seeking to serve God and bring honor to my parents by being the godly young man that Scripture describes?

"I have written unto you, fathers, because ye have known him that is from the beginning. I have written unto you, young men, because ye are strong, and the word of God abideth in you, and ye have overcome the wicked one." *(1 John 2:14)*

"Young men likewise exhort to be sober minded. In all things shewing thyself a pattern of good works: in doctrine shewing uncorruptness, gravity, sincerity, Sound speech, that cannot be condemned; that he that is of the contrary part may be ashamed, having no evil thing to say of you." *(Titus 2:6-8)*

"Wherewithal shall a young man cleanse his way? by taking heed thereto according to thy word. With my whole heart have I sought thee: O let me not wander from thy commandments." *(Psalm 119:9-10)*

I sin against my parents through:
Neglect of the Duties Required Toward Them

If I am careless in fulfilling any of the duties required of me by God toward my parents, I am sinning. God has clearly defined my duties as a son or daughter, and in obedience to Him, and in respect for my parents, I must be diligent to fulfill those duties.

Am I bringing glory to God by faithfully serving and fulfilling my duties to my parents?

"If any man speak, let him speak as the oracles of God; if any man minister, let him do it as of the ability which God giveth: that God in all things may be glorified through Jesus Christ, to whom be praise and dominion for ever and ever. Amen." *(1 Peter 4:11)*

"Let your light so shine before men, that they may see your good works, and glorify your Father which is in heaven." *(Matthew 5:16)*

"It is good for a man that he bear the yoke in his youth." *(Lamentations 3:27)*

Am I obeying my parents as to the Lord, seeking to fulfill all that God requires of me and not just what they expect or demand of me?

"And whatsoever ye do, do it heartily, as to the Lord, and not unto men; knowing that of the Lord ye shall receive the reward of the inheritance: for ye serve the Lord Christ." (Colossians 3:23-24)

"Not slothful in business; fervent in spirit; serving the Lord." (Romans 12:11)

"Servants, be obedient to them that are your masters according to the flesh, with fear and trembling, in singleness of your heart, as unto Christ; not with eyeservice, as menpleasers; but as the servants of Christ, doing the will of God from the heart. With good will doing service, as to the Lord, and not to men." (Ephesians 6:5-7)

Do I neglect to show my parents the courtesies that honor their position as my parents?

"Honour thy father and thy mother, as the LORD thy God hath commanded thee; that thy days may be prolonged, and that it may go well with thee, in the land which the LORD thy God giveth thee." (Deuteronomy 5:16)

"Thou shalt rise up before the hoary head, and honour the face of the old man, and fear thy God: I am the LORD." (Leviticus 19:32)

"Put not forth thyself in the presence of the king, and stand not in the place of great men: for better it is that it be said unto thee, Come up hither; than that thou shouldest be put lower in the presence of the prince whom thine eyes have seen." (Proverbs 25:6-7)

Do my words and actions (or lack of them) express ingratitude or disrespect to my parents and to God who gave me my parents?

"Yea, they are greedy dogs which can never have enough, and they are shepherds that cannot understand: they all look to their own way, every one for his gain, from his quarter." (Isaiah 56:11)

"For men shall be lovers of their own selves, covetous, boasters, proud, blasphemers, disobedient to parents, unthankful, unholy, without natural affection, trucebreakers, false accusers, incontinent, fierce, despisers of those that are good, traitors, heady, highminded, lovers of pleasures more than lovers of God; having a form of godliness, but denying the power thereof: from such turn away." (2 Timothy 3:2-5)

Do I neglect to pray for my parents as they lead and care for our family?

"Moreover as for me, God forbid that I should sin against the LORD in ceasing to pray for you: but I will teach you the good and the right way." (1 Samuel 12:23)

"Pray without ceasing." (1 Thessalonians 5:17)

"I exhort therefore, that, first of all, supplications, prayers, intercessions, and giving of thanks, be made for all men; for kings, and for all that are in authority; that we may lead a quiet and peaceable life in all godliness and honesty. For this is good and acceptable in the sight of God our Saviour." (1 Timothy 2:1-3)

Am I dishonest or secretive with my parents? Do I withhold information that they should have?

"Bread of deceit is sweet to a man; but afterwards his mouth shall be filled with gravel." (Proverbs 20:17)

"For God shall bring every work into judgment, with every secret thing, whether it be good, or whether it be evil." (Ecclesiastes 12:14)

Do I withdraw from my parents and family, refusing to communicate in a polite and cheerful manner with them?

"Withhold not good from them to whom it is due, when it is in the power of thine hand to do it." (Proverbs 3:27)

"Be kindly affectioned one to another with brotherly love; in honour preferring one another." (Romans 12:10)

Am I expecting to be served, rather than cheerfully serving in our household?

"He that loveth pleasure shall be a poor man: he that loveth wine and oil shall not be rich." (Proverbs 21:17)

"He that tilleth his land shall have plenty of bread: but he that followeth after vain persons shall have poverty enough." (Proverbs 28:19)

"In all labour there is profit: but the talk of the lips tendeth only to penury." (Proverbs 14:23)

In my laziness, am I stealing the time and energy of others in my family by not doing my share of the work?

"He also that is slothful in his work is brother to him that is a great waster." (Proverbs 18:9)

"As vinegar to the teeth, and as smoke to the eyes, so is the sluggard to them that send him." (Proverbs 10:26)

"Yet a little sleep, a little slumber, a little folding of the hands to sleep: So shall thy poverty come as one that travelleth; and thy want as an armed man." (Proverbs 24:33-34)

"The sluggard is wiser in his own conceit than seven men that can render a reason." (Proverbs 26:16)

"By much slothfulness the building decayeth; and through idleness of the hands the house droppeth through." (Ecclesiastes 10:18)

Do I waste our family's resources?

"He becometh poor that dealeth with a slack hand: but the hand of the diligent maketh rich." (Proverbs 10:4)

"The slothful man roasteth not that which he took in hunting: but the substance of a diligent man is precious." (Proverbs 12:27)

"He that is faithful in that which is least is faithful also in much: and he that is unjust in the least is unjust also in much. If therefore ye have not been faithful in the unrighteous mammon, who will commit to your trust the true riches? And if ye have not been faithful in that which is another man's, who shall give you that which is your own?" (Luke 16:10-12)

"There is treasure to be desired and oil in the dwelling of the wise; but a foolish man spendeth it up." (Proverbs 21:20)

Am I lazy or indifferent in the use and care of family and personal belongings?

"Moreover it is required in stewards, that a man be found faithful." (1 Corinthians 4:2)

"The slothful man roasteth not that which he took in hunting: but the substance of a diligent man is precious." (Proverbs 12:27)

"By much slothfulness the building decayeth; and through idleness of the hands the house droppeth through." (Ecclesiastes 10:18)

"Be thou diligent to know the state of thy flocks, and look well to thy herds. . . And thou shalt have goats' milk enough for thy food, for the food of thy household, and for the maintenance for thy maidens." (Proverbs 27:23 and 27)

"He also that is slothful in his work is brother to him that is a great waster." (Proverbs 18:9)

Is my slothfulness making it more difficult for my parents to fulfill their callings?

"Confidence in an unfaithful man in time of trouble is like a broken tooth, and a foot out of joint." (Proverbs 25:19)

"As vinegar to the teeth, and as smoke to the eyes, so is the sluggard to them that send him." (Proverbs 10:26)

"The way of the slothful man is as an hedge of thorns: but the way of the righteous is made plain." (Proverbs 15:19)

"The heart of her husband doth safely trust in her, so that he shall have no need of spoil." (Proverbs 31:11)

Do I make excuses for my negligence?

"He that observeth the wind shall not sow; and he that regardeth the clouds shall not reap." (Ecclesiastes 11:4)

"In the morning sow thy seed, and in the evening withhold not thine hand: for thou knowest not whether shall prosper, either this or that, or whether they both shall be alike good." (Ecclesiastes 11:6)

"The sluggard will not plow by reason of the cold; therefore shall he beg in harvest, and have nothing." (Proverbs 20:4)

"The slothful man saith, There is a lion without, I shall be slain in the streets." (Proverbs 22:13)

"The sluggard is wiser in his own conceit than seven men that can render a reason." (Proverbs 26:16)

Am I experiencing difficulties in my family that are directly related to my own sin and negligence?

"Slothfulness casteth into a deep sleep; and an idle soul shall suffer hunger." (Proverbs 19:15)

"The way of the slothful man is as an hedge of thorns: but the way of the righteous is made plain." (Proverbs 15:19)

"The hand of the diligent shall bear rule: but the slothful shall be under tribute." (Proverbs 12:24)

"Even as I have seen, they that plow iniquity, and sow wickedness, reap the same." (Job 4:8)

"Your iniquities have turned away these things, and your sins have withholden good things from you." (Jeremiah 5:25)

"Behold, the LORD's hand is not shortened, that it cannot save; neither his ear heavy, that it cannot hear: but your iniquities have separated between you and your God, and your sins have hid his face from you, that he will not hear." (Isaiah 59:1-2)

I sin against my parents by:

Envying at Their Persons and Places

The sin of pride will tempt me to resist my parents' rule over me. I will be tempted to question their right to govern my actions and their ability to make wise decisions on my behalf. In order to quietly rest under the protection and leadership of my parents, I must prayerfully remain in humble submission to God and His sovereign plan.

Do I pray for God to reveal areas of pride and sin in my life?

"Who can understand his errors? cleanse thou me from secret faults." (Psalm 19:12)

"Search me, O God, and know my heart: try me, and know my thoughts: and see if there be any wicked way in me, and lead me in the way everlasting." (Psalm 139:23-24)

"The heart is deceitful above all things, and desperately wicked: who can know it?" (Jeremiah 17:9)

Do I resist or resent my God-ordained position of subordinance under my parents?

"But now hath God set the members every one of them in the body, as it hath pleased him. And if they were all one member, where were the body? But now are they many members, yet but one body. And the eye cannot say unto the hand, I have no need of thee: nor again the head to the feet, I have no need of you." (1 Corinthians 12:18-21)

"Take my yoke upon you, and learn of me; for I am meek and lowly in heart: and ye shall find rest unto your souls." (Matthew 11:29)

Am I challenging the right of my parents to rule over me?

"Let us not be desirous of vain glory, provoking one another, envying one another." (Galatians 5:26)

"Submit yourselves to every ordinance of man for the Lord's sake: whether it be to the king, as supreme; or unto governors, as unto them that are sent by him for the punishment of evildoers, and for the praise of them that do well." (1 Peter 2:13-14)

"Children, obey your parents in the Lord, for this is right." (Ephesians 6:1)

Am I, in pride, stepping out from under the protection of my parents and their loving authority over me?

"Let every soul be subject unto the higher powers. For there is no power but of God: the powers that be are ordained of God. Whosoever therefore resisteth the power, resisteth the ordinance of God: and they that resist shall receive to themselves damnation. For rulers are not a terror to good works, but to the evil. Wilt thou then not be afraid of the power? do that which is good, and thou shalt have praise of the same: for he is the minister of God to thee for good. But if thou do that which is evil, be afraid; for he beareth not the sword in vain: for he is the minister of God, a revenger to execute wrath upon him that doeth evil. Wherefore ye must needs be subject, not only for wrath, but also for conscience sake." (Romans 13:1-5)

"As a bird that wandereth from her nest, so is a man that wandereth from his place." (Proverbs 27:8)

Am I unwilling to trust God to lead me through the counsel, commands, and decisions of my parents?

"Who is a wise man and endued with knowledge among you? let him show out of a good conversation his works with meekness of wisdom. . . But the wisdom that is from above is first pure, then peaceable, gentle, and easy to be entreated, full of mercy and good fruits, without partiality, and without hypocrisy. And the fruit of righteousness is sown in peace of them that make peace." (James 3:13 and 17-18)

"Because I have called, and ye refused; I have stretched out my hand, and no man regarded; but ye have set at nought all my counsel, and would none of my reproof: I also will laugh at your calamity; I will mock when your fear cometh." (Proverbs 1:24-26)

"For he established a testimony in Jacob, and appointed a law in Israel, which he commanded our fathers, that they should make them known to their children: that the generation to come might know them, even the children which should be born; who should arise and declare them to their children: that they might set their hope in God, and not forget the works of God, but keep his commandments." (Psalm 78:5-7)

"Train up a child in the way he should go, and when he is old he will not depart from it." (Proverbs 22:6)

Am I unwilling to submit my will to that of my parents?

"Let every soul be subject unto the higher powers. For there is no power but of God: the powers that be are ordained of God. Whosoever therefore resisteth the power, resisteth the ordinance of God: and they that resist shall receive to themselves damnation." (Romans 13:1-2)

"Likewise, ye younger, submit yourselves unto the elder. Yea, all of you be subject one to another, and be clothed with humility: for God resisteth the proud, and giveth grace to the humble." (1 Peter 5:5)

Am I acting as the authority in my own life?

"The way of a fool is right in his own eyes: but he that hearkeneth unto counsel is wise." (Proverbs 12:15)

"No man can serve two masters, for either he will hate the one, and love the other, or else he will hold to the one, and despise the other. Ye cannot serve God and mammon." (Matthew 6:24)

"There is a way that seemeth right unto a man, but the end thereof are the ways of death." (Proverbs 16:25)

"Keep back thy servant also from presumptuous sins; let them not have dominion over me: then shall I be upright, and I shall be innocent from the great transgression." (Psalm 19:13)

Do I argue with my parents?

"From whence come wars and fightings among you? come they not hence, even of your lusts that war in your members? Ye lust, and have not: ye kill, and desire to have, and cannot obtain: ye fight and war, yet ye have not, because ye ask not." (James 4:1-2)

"The beginning of strife is as when one letteth out water: therefore leave off contention, before it be meddled with." (Proverbs 17:14)

"He is proud, knowing nothing, but doting about questions and strifes of words, whereof cometh envy, strife, railings, evil surmisings, perverse disputings of men of corrupt minds, and destitute of the truth, supposing that gain is godliness: from such withdraw thyself." (1 Timothy 6:4-5)

Am I angry when my parents' decisions go against my will?

"An angry man stirreth up strife, and a furious man aboundeth in transgression." (Proverbs 29:22)

"A wrathful man stirreth up strife: but he that is slow to anger appeaseth strife." (Proverbs 15:18)

"For where envying and strife is, there is confusion and every evil work." (James 3:16)

"He that is soon angry dealeth foolishly: and a man of wicked devices is hated." (Proverb 14:17)

"Proud and haughty scorner is his name, who dealeth in proud wrath." (Proverbs 21:24)

Is my relationship with my parents one of mutual encouragement and respect, or one of strife and discord?

"For ye are yet carnal: for whereas there is among you envying, and strife, and divisions, are ye not carnal, and walk as men?" (1 Corinthians 3:3)

"Strive not with a man without cause, if he have done thee no harm." (Proverbs 3:30)

"A sound heart is the life of the flesh: but envy the rottenness of the bones." (Proverbs 14:30)

"Honour thy father and thy mother: that thy days may be long upon the land which the LORD thy God giveth thee." (Exodus 20:12)

Do I seek to exercise authority that is not rightfully mine in our household?

"For if a man think himself to be something, when he is nothing, he deceiveth himself." (Galatians 6:3)

"He loveth transgression that loveth strife: and he that exalteth his gate seeketh destruction." (Proverbs 17:19)

"For I say, through the grace given unto me, to every man that is among you, not to think of himself more highly than he ought to think; but to think soberly, according as God hath dealt to every man the measure of faith." (Romans 12:3)

"Knowledge puffeth up, but charity edifieth. And if any man think that he knoweth any thing, he knoweth nothing yet as he ought to know." (1 Corinthians 8:1b-2)

Do I seek to discredit my parents' ability to lead me and our family?

"Whoso privily slandereth his neighbour, him will I cut off: him that hath an high look and a proud heart will not I suffer." (Psalm 101:5)

"Let nothing be done through strife or vainglory; but in lowliness of mind let each esteem other better than themselves." (Philippians 2:3)

"But if ye have bitter envying and strife in your hearts, glory not, and lie not against the truth. This wisdom descendeth not from above, but is earthly, sensual, devilish. For where envying and strife is, there is confusion and every evil work." (James 3:14-16)

Do I criticize the actions and decisions my parents make related to me and my siblings?

"He that passeth by, and meddleth with strife belonging not to him, is like one that taketh a dog by the ears." (Proverbs 26:17)

"But if ye bite and devour one another, take heed that ye be not consumed one of another." (Galatians 5:15)

"The Lord knoweth how to deliver the godly out of temptations, and to reserve the unjust unto the day of judgment to be punished: but chiefly them that walk after the flesh in the lust of uncleanness, and despise government. Presumptuous are they, selfwilled, they are not afraid to speak evil of dignities." (2 Peter 2:9-10)

Do I attempt to draw my siblings' loyalty away from my parents and toward me?

"Let us not be desirous of vain glory, provoking one another, envying one another." (Galatians 5:26)

"Now I beseech you, brethren, mark them which cause divisions and offences contrary to the doctrine which ye have learned; and avoid them. For they that are such serve not our Lord Jesus Christ, but their own belly; and by good words and fair speeches deceive the hearts of the simple. For your obedience is come abroad unto all men. I am glad therefore on your behalf: but yet I would have you wise unto that which is good, and simple concerning evil." (Romans 16:17-19)

"Absalom said moreover, Oh that I were made judge in the land, that every man which hath any suit or cause might come unto me, and I would do him justice! And it was so, that when any man came nigh to him to do him obeisance, he put forth his hand, and took him, and kissed him. And on this manner did Absalom to all Israel that came to the king for judgment: so Absalom stole the hearts of the men of Israel." (2 Samuel 15:4-6)

Do I seek to lead my siblings in a direction that is contrary to the goals and leadership of my parents?

"It is an honour for a man to cease from strife: but every fool will be meddling." (Proverbs 20:3)

"But let none of you suffer as a murderer, or as a thief, or as an evildoer, or as a busybody in other men's matters." (1 Peter 4:15)

"And that ye study to be quiet, and to do your own business, and to work with your own hands, as we commanded you." (1 Thessalonians 4:11)

Do I challenge the authority and character of my parents when they abuse or neglect their responsibilities, fearing that God has forgotten me or is powerless to help?

"Hatred stirreth up strifes: but love covereth all sins." (Proverbs 10:12)

"Let your conversation be without covetousness; and be content with such things as ye have: for he hath said, I will never leave thee, nor forsake thee." (Hebrews 13:5)

"I therefore, the prisoner of the Lord, beseech you that ye walk worthy of the vocation wherewith ye are called, with all lowliness and meekness, with longsuffering, forbearing one another in love; endeavouring to keep the unity of the Spirit in the bond of peace." (Ephesians 4:1-3)

"The LORD hath been mindful of us: he will bless us…" (Psalm 115:12a)

"And Moses said unto the people, Fear ye not, stand still, and see the salvation of the LORD, which he will shew to you to day…" (Exodus 14:13a)

I sin against my parents through:

Contempt of Their Persons and Places

I cannot hold my parents in contempt while obeying God's command to honor them. As I honor my parents, I will acknowledge their worth and their rank as it has been granted by God. To despise them implies that I view them as worthless and below myself. The prideful attitude of contempt will express itself in actions, attitudes, and words that must be repented of.

Do I treat my parents disrespectfully?

"He that wasteth his father, and chaseth away his mother, is a son that causeth shame, and bringeth reproach." (Proverbs 19:26)

"Honour thy father and thy mother: that thy days may be long upon the land which the LORD thy God giveth thee." (Exodus 20:12)

Do my face and gestures communicate sinful pride toward my parents?

"An high look, and a proud heart, and the plowing of the wicked, is sin." (Proverbs 21:4)

"A wicked man hardeneth his face: but as for the upright, he directeth his way." (Proverbs 21:29)

Do I, in self-righteous pride, criticize my parents for their alleged faults and sins?

"When pride cometh, then cometh shame: but with the lowly is wisdom." (Proverbs 11:2)

"Thou hypocrite, first cast out the beam out of thine own eye; and then shalt thou see clearly to cast out the mote out of thy brother's eye." (Matthew 7:5)

"Is it fit to say to a king, Thou art wicked? and to princes, Ye are ungodly?" (Job 34:18)

Has my sinful pride led me to set myself up as the judge of my parents?

"Judge not, that ye be not judged. For with what judgment ye judge, ye shall be judged: and with what measure ye mete, it shall be measured to you again. And why beholdest thou the mote that is in thy brother's eye, but considerest not the beam that is in thine own eye?" (Matthew 7:1-3)

"When pride cometh, then cometh shame: but with the lowly is wisdom." (Proverbs 11:2)

"But chiefly them that walk after the flesh in the lust of uncleanness, and despise government. Presumptuous are they, selfwilled, they are not afraid to speak evil of dignities." (2 Peter 2:10)

"There is a generation that are pure in their own eyes, and yet is not washed from their filthiness. There is a generation, O how lofty are their eyes! and their eyelids are lifted up." (Proverbs 30:12-13)

Do I seek to find fault with my parents and their ideas, opinions, decisions, teaching, habits, dress, friendships, family, etc.?

". . . Knowledge puffeth up, but charity edifieth." (1 Corinthians 8:1b)

"[Charity] doth not behave itself unseemly, seeketh not her own, is not easily provoked, thinketh no evil." (1 Corinthians 13:5)

"The soul of the wicked desireth evil: his neighbour findeth no favour in his eyes." (Proverbs 21:10)

"But why dost thou judge thy brother? or why dost thou set at nought thy brother? for we shall all stand before the judgment seat of Christ." (Romans 14:10)

Do I recognize that God will judge me for my pride and disrespect?

"Be not deceived; God is not mocked: for whatsoever a man soweth, that shall he also reap. For he that soweth to his flesh shall of the flesh reap corruption; but he that soweth to the Spirit shall of the Spirit reap life everlasting." (Galatians 6:7-8)

"Whoso privily slandereth his neighbour, him will I cut off: him that hath an high look and a proud heart will not I suffer." (Psalm 101:5)

"Surely he scorneth the scorners: but he giveth grace unto the lowly." (Proverbs 3:34)

"Pride goeth before destruction, and an haughty spirit before a fall." (Proverbs 16:18)

"For the day of the LORD of hosts shall be upon every one that is proud and lofty, and upon every one that is lifted up; and he shall be brought low." (Isaiah 2:12)

Am I actively seeking in my actions, speech, dress, music, or hairstyle to displease my parents?

"The soul of the wicked desireth evil: his neighbour findeth no favour in his eyes." (Proverbs 21:10)

"An evil man seeketh only rebellion: therefore a cruel messenger shall be sent against him." (Proverbs 17:11)

Do I compare my parents unfavorably with other parents?

"Thou shalt not covet thy neighbour's house, thou shalt not covet thy neighbour's wife, nor his manservant, nor his maidservant, nor his ox, nor his ass, nor any thing that is thy neighbour's." (Exodus 20:17)

Am I ashamed and embarrassed by my parents? Do I worry about what others think and seek to protect my own reputation?

"I sought the LORD, and he heard me, and delivered me from all my fears. They looked unto him, and were lightened: and their faces were not ashamed." (Psalm 34:4-5)

"Let nothing be done through strife or vainglory; but in lowliness of mind let each esteem other better than themselves." (Philippians 2:3)

"Pride goeth before destruction, and an haughty spirit before a fall. Better it is to be of an humble spirit with the lowly, than to divide the spoil with the proud." (Proverbs 16:18-19)

"But why dost thou judge thy brother? or why dost thou set at nought thy brother? for we shall all stand before the judgment seat of Christ." (Romans 14:10)

Do I keep company with others who do not respect their parents?

"Make no friendship with an angry man; and with a furious man thou shalt not go: lest thou learn his ways, and get a snare to thy soul." (Proverbs 22:24-25)

"Can two walk together, except they be agreed?" (Amos 3:3)

"My son, if sinners entice thee, consent thou not." (Proverbs 1:10)

Do I say things to others that would lead them to false conclusions about my parents?

"Be not a witness against thy neighbour without cause; and deceive not with thy lips." (Proverbs 24:28)

"A false witness shall not be unpunished, and he that speaketh lies shall perish." (Proverbs 19:9)

"My lips shall not speak wickedness, nor my tongue utter deceit." (Job 27:4)

"A righteous man hateth lying: but a wicked man is loathsome, and cometh to shame." (Proverbs 13:5)

Do I speak evil of my parents to others?

"Then said Paul, I wist not, brethren, that he was the high priest: for it is written, Thou shalt not speak evil of the ruler of thy people." (Acts 23:5)

"Whoso privily slandereth his neighbour, him will I cut off: him that hath an high look and a proud heart will not I suffer." (Psalm 101:5)

"The Lord knoweth how to deliver the godly out of temptations, and to reserve the unjust unto the day of judgment to be punished: But chiefly them that walk after the flesh in the lust of uncleanness, and despise government. Presumptuous are they, selfwilled, they are not afraid to speak evil of dignities." (2 Peter 2:9-10)

"The fear of the LORD is to hate evil: pride, and arrogancy, and the evil way, and the froward mouth, do I hate." (Proverbs 8:13)

Is my heart bitter and resentful toward my parents?

"Looking diligently lest any man fail of the grace of God; lest any root of bitterness springing up trouble you, and thereby many be defiled." (Hebrews 12:15)

"Thou shalt not avenge, nor bear any grudge against the children of thy people, but thou shalt love thy neighbour as thyself: I am the LORD." (Leviticus 19:18)

"Let all bitterness, and wrath, and anger, and clamour, and evil speaking, be put away from you, with all malice: and be ye kind one to another, tenderhearted, forgiving one another, even as God for Christ's sake hath forgiven you." (Ephesians 4:31-32)

Am I bitterly resistant to my parents' attempts to lead and teach me?

"Whosoever therefore resisteth the power, resisteth the ordinance of God: and they that resist shall receive to themselves damnation. For rulers are not a terror to good works, but to the evil. Wilt thou then not be afraid of the power? do that which is good, and thou shalt have praise of the same: for he is the minister of God to thee for good. But if thou do that which is evil, be afraid; for he beareth not the sword in vain: for he is the minister of God, a revenger to execute wrath upon him that doeth evil." (Romans 13:2-4)

"He therefore that despiseth, despiseth not man, but God, who hath also given unto us his holy Spirit." (1 Thessalonians 4:8)

Do I despise my parents and the authority they exercise over me?

"Hearken unto thy father that begat thee, and despise not thy mother when she is old." (Proverbs 23:22)

"He that saith he is in the light, and hateth his brother, is in darkness even until now. He that loveth his brother abideth in the light, and there is none occasion of stumbling in him. But he that hateth his brother is in darkness, and walketh in darkness, and knoweth not whither he goeth, because that darkness hath blinded his eyes." (1 John 2:9-11)

"Thou shalt not hate thy brother in thine heart: thou shalt in any wise rebuke thy neighbour, and not suffer sin upon him." (Leviticus 19:17)

"And this commandment have we from him, That he who loveth God love his brother also." (1 John 4:21)

"Whosoever hateth his brother is a murderer: and ye know that no murderer hath eternal life abiding in him." (1 John 3:15)

"He that is void of wisdom despiseth his neighbour: but a man of understanding holdeth his peace." (Proverbs 11:12)

Do I speak words of bitterness, sarcasm, and hatred to my parents?

"How long will ye vex my soul, and break me in pieces with words?" (Job 19:2)

"Let the words of my mouth, and the meditation of my heart, be acceptable in thy sight, O LORD, my strength, and my redeemer." (Psalm 19:14)

"Hide me from the secret counsel of the wicked; from the insurrection of the workers of iniquity: who whet their tongue like a sword, and bend their bows to shoot their arrows, even bitter words: that they may shoot in secret at the perfect: suddenly do they shoot at him, and fear not." (Psalm 64:2-4)

Is my sinful attitude contributing to a spirit of strife and contention in our home?

"Cast out the scorner, and contention shall go out; yea, strife and reproach shall cease." (Proverbs 22:10)

"Scoffers set a city aflame, but wise men turn away wrath." (Proverbs 29:8, NKJV)

"He that is of a proud heart stirreth up strife: but he that putteth his trust in the LORD shall be made fat." (Proverbs 28:25)

"From whence come wars and fightings among you? come they not hence, even of your lusts that war in your members?" (James 4:1)

"These six things doth the LORD hate: yea, seven are an abomination unto him: a proud look, a lying tongue, and hands that shed innocent blood, an heart that deviseth wicked imaginations, feet that be swift in running to mischief, a false witness that speaketh lies, and he that soweth discord among brethren." (Proverbs 6:16-19)

Do I seek to hurt my parents with my words and actions?

"There is that speaketh like the piercings of a sword: but the tongue of the wise is health." (Proverbs 12:18)

"It is as sport to a fool to do mischief: but a man of understanding hath wisdom." (Proverbs 10:23)

"A froward man soweth strife: and a whisperer separateth chief friends." (Proverbs 16:28)

Is my bitter attitude tempting my parents to be discouraged or angry?

"For it was not an enemy that reproached me; then I could have borne it: neither was it he that hated me that did magnify himself against me; then I would have hid myself from him." (Psalm 55:12)

"Let us not therefore judge one another any more: but judge this rather, that no man put a stumblingblock or an occasion to fall in his brother's way." (Romans 14:13)

Am I seeking to avenge myself of the wrongs my parents have allegedly committed against me?

"Follow peace with all men, and holiness, without which no man shall see the Lord." (Hebrews 12:14)

"He was oppressed, and he was afflicted, yet he opened not his mouth: he is brought as a lamb to the slaughter, and as a sheep before her shearers is dumb, so he openeth not his mouth." (Isaiah 53:7)

"Fret not thyself because of evil men, neither be thou envious at the wicked." (Proverbs 24:19)

"Dearly beloved, avenge not yourselves, but rather give place unto wrath: for it is written, Vengeance is mine; I will repay, saith the Lord. Therefore if thine enemy hunger, feed him; if he thirst, give him drink: for in so doing thou shalt heap coals of fire on his head. Be not overcome of evil, but overcome evil with good." (Romans 12:19-21)

"If a man say, I love God, and hateth his brother, he is a liar: for he that loveth not his brother whom he hath seen, how can he love God whom he hath not seen?" (1 John 4:20)

Am I responding to the Holy Spirit and to God's Word which call me to repent and turn from my sinful attitude of contempt toward my parents and their leadership?

"As many as I love, I rebuke and chasten: be zealous therefore, and repent." (Revelation 3:19)

"For the wrath of man worketh not the righteousness of God. Wherefore lay apart all filthiness and superfluity of naughtiness, and receive with meekness the engrafted word, which is able to save your souls. But be ye doers of the word, and not hearers only, deceiving your own selves." (James 1:20-22)

"...that they should repent and turn to God, and do works meet for repentance." (Acts 26:20b)

I sin against my parents through:

Rebellion against Their Lawful Counsels

True reverence for my parents will lead to an eagerness to hear and follow their counsels. I will acknowledge their greater wisdom. I will be grateful for their direction. I will recognize their role as God's appointed leaders in my life, and will submit myself to their counsel. If I am rejecting their guidance, I am rejecting God's guidance, and rebelling against Him.

Do I consider myself wise enough to live a life that pleases God without the godly counsel of others?

"Do not be wise in your own eyes; fear the LORD and turn away from evil. It will be healing to your body, and refreshment to your bones." (Proverbs 3:7-8, NASB)

"Every way of a man is right in his own eyes: but the LORD pondereth the hearts." (Proverbs 21:2)

"For if a man think himself to be something, when he is nothing, he deceiveth himself." (Galatians 6:3)

"He that trusteth in his own heart is a fool: but whoso walketh wisely, he shall be delivered." (Proverbs 28:26)

Am I impatiently unwilling to seek the counsel of others before making important decisions?

"The thoughts of the diligent tend only to plenteousness; but of every one that is hasty only to want." (Proverbs 21:5)

"Also, that the soul be without knowledge, it is not good; and he that hasteth with his feet sinneth." (Proverbs 19:2)

Do my parents feel free to offer me honest counsel, or am I defensive or resistant to their advice and direction?

"A fool does not delight in understanding, but only in revealing his own mind." (Proverbs 18:2, NASB)

"There is a way that seemeth right unto a man, but the end thereof are the ways of death." (Proverbs 16:25)

"Every prudent man dealeth with knowledge: but a fool layeth open his folly." (Proverbs 13:16)

Do I ignore my parents when they attempt to offer me counsel?

"A wise man will hear, and will increase learning; and a man of understanding shall attain unto wise counsels." (Proverbs 1:5)

"My son, hear the instruction of thy father, and forsake not the law of thy mother." (Proverbs 1:8)

"Hear, O my son, and receive my sayings; and the years of thy life shall be many." (Proverbs 4:10)

"Hear counsel, and receive instruction, that thou mayest be wise in thy latter end." (Proverbs 19:20)

"Bow down thine ear, and hear the words of the wise, and apply thine heart unto my knowledge." (Proverbs 22:17)

Do I treat my parents' opinions as unimportant, inconsequential, or foolish?

"But ye have set at nought all my counsel, and would none of my reproof." (Proverbs 1:25)

"If thou be wise, thou shalt be wise for thyself: but if thou scornest, thou alone shalt bear it." (Proverbs 9:12)

"Seest thou a man wise in his own conceit? there is more hope of a fool than of him." (Proverbs 26:12)

"The sluggard is wiser in his own conceit than seven men that can render a reason." (Proverbs 26:16)

Am I unwilling to listen to and prayerfully submit to the counsel of my parents?

"He that refuseth instruction despiseth his own soul: but he that heareth reproof getteth understanding." (Proverbs 15:32)

"He that answereth a matter before he heareth it, it is folly and shame unto him." (Proverbs 18:13)

"Hear instruction, and be wise, and refuse it not." (Proverbs 8:33)

"But they hearkened not, nor inclined their ear, but walked in the counsels and in the imagination of their evil heart, and went backward, and not forward." (Jeremiah 7:24)

"The man that wandereth out of the way of understanding shall remain in the congregation of the dead." (Proverbs 21:16)

Do I communicate with my face and body an attitude of stubbornness and indifference when my parents seek to guide me?

"The wicked, through the pride of his countenance, will not seek after God: God is not in all his thoughts." (Psalm 10:4)

"An high look, and a proud heart, and the plowing of the wicked, is sin." (Proverbs 21:4)

"And the afflicted people thou wilt save: but thine eyes are upon the haughty, that thou mayest bring them down." (2 Samuel 22:28)

Do I resent my parents' efforts to guide me?

"A fool despiseth his father's instruction: but he that regardeth reproof is prudent." (Proverbs 15:5)

"Because that, when they knew God, they glorified him not as God, neither were thankful; but became vain in their imaginations, and their foolish heart was darkened. Professing themselves to be wise, they became fools." (Romans 1:21-22)

"O Jerusalem, Jerusalem, thou that killest the prophets, and stonest them which are sent unto thee, how often would I have gathered thy children together, even as a hen gathereth her chickens under her wings, and ye would not!" (Matthew 23:37)

Do I respond in anger to my parents' counsel and guidance?

"A fool despiseth his father's instruction: but he that regardeth reproof is prudent." (Proverbs 15:5)

"A fool's wrath is presently known: but a prudent man covereth shame." (Proverbs 12:16)

"Be not hasty in thy spirit to be angry: for anger resteth in the bosom of fools." (Ecclesiastes 7:9)

"He that hath knowledge spareth his words: and a man of understanding is of an excellent spirit. Even a fool, when he holdeth his peace, is counted wise: and he that shutteth his lips is esteemed a man of understanding." (Proverbs 17:27-28)

Do I argue against the godly advice of my parents?

"He who separates himself seeks his own desire, he quarrels against all sound wisdom." (Proverbs 18:1, NASB)

"Keeping away from strife is an honor for a man, but any fool will quarrel." (Proverbs 20:3, NASB)

"Even a fool, when he holdeth his peace, is counted wise: and he that shutteth his lips is esteemed a man of understanding." (Proverbs 17:28)

Do I seek and prefer the counsel of my friends over that of my parents?

"It is better to hear the rebuke of the wise, than for a man to hear the song of fools." (Ecclesiastes 7:5)

"He that walketh with wise men shall be wise: but a companion of fools shall be destroyed." (Proverbs 13:20)

Do I seek or honor advice from others, godly or ungodly, that will be contrary to my parents' lawful counsel?

"My son, fear thou the LORD and the king: and meddle not with them that are given to change. For their calamity shall rise suddenly; and who knoweth the ruin of them both?" (Proverbs 24:21-22)

"Wisdom is before him that hath understanding; but the eyes of a fool are in the ends of the earth." (Proverbs 17:24)

"Cease, my son, to hear the instruction that causeth to err from the words of knowledge." (Proverbs 19:27)

"Blessed is the man that walketh not in the counsel of the ungodly, nor standeth in the way of sinners, nor sitteth in the seat of the scornful." (Psalm 1:1)

Do I refuse to ask my parents for counsel even when I know I need their help?

"Without counsel purposes are disappointed: but in the multitude of counsellers they are established." (Proverbs 15:22)

"A scorner loveth not one that reproveth him: neither will he go unto the wise." (Proverbs 15:12)

After acknowledging the wisdom of my parents' counsel, do I still reject it and follow my own wisdom?

"But be ye doers of the word, and not hearers only, deceiving your own selves. For if any be a hearer of the word, and not a doer, he is like unto a man beholding his natural face in a glass: for he beholdeth himself, and goeth his way, and straightway forgetteth what manner of man he was. But whoso looketh into the perfect law of liberty, and continueth therein, he being not a forgetful hearer, but a doer of the work, this man shall be blessed in his deed." (James 1:22-25)

"Wherefore is there a price in the hand of a fool to get wisdom, seeing he hath no heart to it?" (Proverbs 17:16)

"As a dog returneth to his vomit, so a fool returneth to his folly. Seest thou a man wise in his own conceit? there is more hope of a fool than of him. (Proverbs 26:11-12)

Am I refusing to accept God's guidance as it is directed to me through my parents?

"My son, keep thy father's commandment, and forsake not the law of thy mother: bind them continually upon thine heart, and tie them about thy neck. When thou goest, it shall lead thee; when thou sleepest, it shall keep thee; and when thou awakest, it shall talk with thee. For the commandment is a lamp; and the law is light; and reproofs of instruction are the way of life." (Proverbs 6:20-23)

"For this God is our God for ever and ever: he will be our guide even unto death." (Psalm 48:14)

"I will instruct thee and teach thee in the way which thou shalt go: I will guide thee with mine eye." (Psalm 32:8)

"The meek will he guide in judgment: and the meek will he teach his way." (Psalm 25:9)

Have my parents become discouraged in their efforts to guide me? Are they withholding their counsel because they realize I will reject it?

"He hath said in his heart, God hath forgotten: he hideth his face; he will never see it." (Psalm 10:11)

"Answer a fool as his folly deserves, lest he be wise in his own eyes." (Proverbs 26:5, NASB)

"If a wise man contendeth with a foolish man, whether he rage or laugh, there is no rest." (Proverbs 29:9)

"Give not that which is holy unto the dogs, neither cast ye your pearls before swine, lest they trample them under their feet, and turn again and rend you." (Matthew 7:6)

Do I refuse to believe God's promises of affliction and cursing for those who reject wise counsel?

"Because I have called, and ye refused; I have stretched out my hand, and no man regarded; but ye have set at nought all my counsel, and would none of my reproof: I also will laugh at your calamity; I will mock when your fear cometh; when your fear cometh as desolation, and your destruction cometh as a whirlwind; when distress and anguish cometh upon you. Then shall they call upon me, but I will not answer; they shall seek me early, but they shall not find me: for that they hated knowledge, and did not choose the fear of the LORD: they would none of my counsel: they despised all my reproof. Therefore shall they eat of the fruit of their own way, and be filled with their own devices. For the turning away of the simple shall slay them, and the prosperity of fools shall destroy them. But whoso hearkeneth unto me shall dwell safely, and shall be quiet from fear of evil." (Proverbs 1:24-33)

"Because they rebelled against the words of God, and contemned the counsel of the most High: therefore he brought down their heart with labour; they fell down, and there was none to help." (Psalm 107:11-12)

Does my life reflect the negative results of rejecting instruction and counsel?

"Good understanding giveth favour: but the way of transgressors is hard." (Proverbs 13:15)

"I am the LORD thy God, which brought thee out of the land of Egypt: open thy mouth wide, and I will fill it. But my people would not hearken to my voice; and Israel would none of me. So I gave them up unto their own hearts' lust: and they walked in their own counsels. Oh that my people had hearkened unto me, and Israel had walked in my ways! I should soon have subdued their enemies, and turned my hand against their adversaries. The haters of the LORD should have submitted themselves unto him: but their time should have endured for ever. He should have fed them also with the finest of the wheat: and with honey out of the rock should I have satisfied thee." (Psalm 81:10-16)

"Because they rebelled against the words of God, and contemned the counsel of the most High: therefore he brought down their heart with labour; they fell down, and there was none to help." (Psalm 107:11-12)

If my parents offer counsel that is contrary to God's Word, do I humbly appeal to them, or do I self-righteously criticize and reject their words?

"Likewise, ye younger, submit yourselves unto the elder. Yea, all of you be subject one to another, and be clothed with humility: for God resisteth the proud, and giveth grace to the humble. Humble yourselves therefore under the mighty hand of God, that he may exalt you in due time: casting all your care upon him; for he careth for you." (1 Peter 5:5-7)

"Brethren, if a man be overtaken in a fault, ye which are spiritual, restore such an one in the spirit of meekness; considering thyself, lest thou also be tempted." (Galatians 6:1)

I sin against my parents through:

Rebellion against Their Lawful Commands

I am not honoring my parents when I choose to disobey them. God promises that it will not "go well" with me when I disobey Him by disobeying my parents. I must remember that anything other than immediate and thorough obedience to their commands is disobedience. I must resist the temptation to argue, procrastinate, complain, or negotiate, and I must pray for a heart that will cheerfully rejoice at every opportunity to carry out my parents' commands.

Do I recognize that rebellion against my parents' lawful commands is rebellion against God who has placed my parents over me?

"Let every soul be subject unto the higher powers. For there is no power but of God: the powers that be are ordained of God. Whosoever therefore resisteth the power, resisteth the ordinance of God: and they that resist shall receive to themselves damnation." (Romans 13:1-2)

"Jesus answered, Thou couldest have no power at all against me, except it were given thee from above. . ." (John 19:11a)

When my parents tell me to do something, do I grumble and complain?

"Do all things without murmurings and disputings." (Philippians 2:14)

"A fool's lips enter into contention, and his mouth calleth for strokes." (Proverbs 18:6)

". . . Your murmurings are not against us, but against the LORD." (Exodus 16:8b)

"Yea, they despised the pleasant land, they believed not his word: but murmured in their tents, and hearkened not unto the voice of the LORD. Therefore he lifted up his hand against them, to overthrow them in the wilderness." (Psalm 106:24-26)

"Do not grumble against one another, brethren, lest you be condemned. Behold, the Judge is standing at the door!" (James 5:9, NKJV)

"It is good for a man that he bear the yoke in his youth." (Lamentations 3:27)

Do I spend a great deal of time discussing an assigned task with my parents without then completing the task?

"In all labour there is profit: but the talk of the lips tendeth only to penury." (Proverbs 14:23)

"A fool also multiplies words. No man knows what is to be; who can tell him what will be after him?" (Ecclesiastes 10:14, NKJV)

Am I careless in the way I complete the tasks that I am given by my parents?

"Not slothful in business; fervent in spirit; serving the Lord." (Romans 12:11)

"He also that is slothful in his work is brother to him that is a great waster." (Proverbs 18:9)

"And whatsoever ye do, do it heartily, as to the Lord, and not unto men; knowing that of the Lord ye shall receive the reward of the inheritance: for ye serve the Lord Christ." (Colossians 3:23-24)

"Whatsoever thy hand findeth to do, do it with thy might; for there is no work, nor device, nor knowledge, nor wisdom, in the grave, whither thou goest." (Ecclesiastes 9:10)

Instead of obeying my parents, do I argue or attempt to negotiate with them?

"In the multitude of words there wanteth not sin: but he that refraineth his lips is wise." (Proverbs 10:19)

"He loveth transgression that loveth strife: and he that exalteth his gate seeketh destruction." (Proverbs 17:19)

"As coals are to burning coals, and wood to fire; so is a contentious man to kindle strife." (Proverbs 26:21)

"He that is of a proud heart stirreth up strife: but he that putteth his trust in the LORD shall be made fat." (Proverbs 28:25)

"For where envying and strife is, there is confusion and every evil work." (James 3:16)

"Only by pride cometh contention: but with the well advised is wisdom." (Proverbs 13:10)

Do I ignore or pretend not to hear my parents when they are giving me instructions?

"The wise in heart will receive commandments: but a prating fool shall fall." (Proverbs 10:8)

"He that turneth away his ear from hearing the law, even his prayer shall be abomination." (Proverbs 28:9)

"My son, attend to my words; incline thine ear unto my sayings." (Proverbs 4:20)

When my parents tell me to do something, do I wait or wrongfully do other things before carrying out their instructions?

"I thought on my ways, and turned my feet unto thy testimonies. I made haste, and delayed not to keep thy commandments." (Psalm 119:59-60)

"Boast not thyself of to morrow; for thou knowest not what a day may bring forth." (Proverbs 27:1)

Do I acknowledge my parents' commands, and then seek ways to avoid obeying them?

"Wherefore the Lord said, Forasmuch as this people draw near me with their mouth, and with their lips do honour me, but have removed their heart far from me, and their fear toward me is taught by the precept of men." (Isaiah 29:13)

"But be ye doers of the word, and not hearers only, deceiving your own selves." (James 1:22)

Do I respond to my parents' authority with anger and resentment?

"Let all bitterness, and wrath, and anger, and clamour, and evil speaking, be put away from you, with all malice: and be ye kind one to another, tenderhearted, forgiving one another, even as God for Christ's sake hath forgiven you." (Ephesians 4:31-32)

"He that is soon angry dealeth foolishly: and a man of wicked devices is hated." (Proverbs 14:17)

"Strive not with a man without cause, if he have done thee no harm." (Proverbs 3:30)

Do I fail to complete the tasks that I have been assigned?

Confidence in an unfaithful man in time of trouble is like a broken tooth, and a foot out of joint." (Proverbs 25:19)

"As vinegar to the teeth, and as smoke to the eyes, so is the sluggard to them that send him." (Proverbs 10:26)

"He that sendeth a message by the hand of a fool cutteth off the feet, and drinketh damage." (Proverbs 26:6)

Do I make excuses for myself when I fail to carry out my parents' commands?

"The slothful man saith, There is a lion in the way; a lion is in the streets." (Proverbs 26:13)

"The sluggard is wiser in his own conceit than seven men that can render a reason." (Proverbs 26:16)

"Every way of a man is right in his own eyes: but the LORD pondereth the hearts." (Proverbs 21:2)

"Confess your faults one to another, and pray one for another, that ye may be healed. The effectual fervent prayer of a righteous man availeth much." (James 5:16)

"If thou sayest, Behold, we knew it not; doth not he that pondereth the heart consider it? and he that keepeth thy soul, doth not he know it? and shall not he render to every man according to his works?" (Proverbs 24:12)

Do I seek to do other things for my parents while failing to follow their clear commands?

"To do justice and judgment is more acceptable to the LORD than sacrifice. An high look, and a proud heart, and the plowing of the wicked, is sin." (Proverbs 21:3-4)

"And Samuel said, Hath the LORD as great delight in burnt offerings and sacrifices, as in obeying the voice of the LORD? Behold, to obey is better than sacrifice, and to hearken than the fat of rams. For rebellion is as the sin of witchcraft, and stubbornness is as iniquity and idolatry. Because thou hast rejected the word of the LORD, he hath also rejected thee from being king." (1 Samuel 15:22-23)

Am I neglecting duties that are clearly mine while busying myself with other activities that are not my responsibility?

"For we hear that there are some which walk among you disorderly, working not at all, but are busybodies. Now them that are such we command and exhort by our Lord Jesus Christ, that with quietness they work, and eat their own bread." (2 Thessalonians 3:11-12)

"And withal they learn to be idle, wandering about from house to house; and not only idle, but tattlers also and busybodies, speaking things which they ought not." (1 Timothy 5:13)

"Submit yourselves to every ordinance of man for the Lord's sake: whether it be to the king, as supreme; or unto governors, as unto them that are sent by him for the punishment of evildoers, and for the praise of them that do well." (1 Peter 2:13-14)

Do I wait to be disciplined for disobedience before I will do what my parents have told me to do?

"Be ye not as the horse, or as the mule, which have no understanding: whose mouth must be held in with bit and bridle, lest they come near unto thee." (Psalm 32:9)

Am I choosing to continue in disobedience to my parents because they fail to discipline when I disobey?

"Every one that is proud in heart is an abomination to the LORD: though hand join in hand, he shall not be unpunished." (Proverbs 16:5)

"The soul that sinneth, it shall die. The son shall not bear the iniquity of the father, neither shall the father bear the iniquity of the son: the righteousness of the righteous shall be upon him, and the wickedness of the wicked shall be upon him." (Ezekiel 18:20)

"Because sentence against an evil work is not executed speedily, therefore the heart of the sons of men is fully set in them to do evil." (Ecclesiastes 8:11)

Do I stubbornly refuse to obey my parents' commands?

"He who keeps the commandment keeps his soul, but he who is careless of his ways will die." (Proverb 19:16, NASB)

"But they and our fathers dealt proudly, and hardened their necks, and hearkened not to thy commandments, And refused to obey, neither were mindful of thy wonders that thou didst among them; but hardened their necks, and in their rebellion appointed a captain to return to their bondage: but thou art a God ready to pardon, gracious and merciful, slow to anger, and of great kindness, and forsookest them not." (Nehemiah 9:16-17)

Do I purposely go against the rules of our household?

"Happy is the man that feareth alway: but he that hardeneth his heart shall fall into mischief." (Proverbs 28:14)

"A worthless person, a wicked man, is the one who walks with a false mouth, who winks with his eyes, who signals with his feet, who points with his fingers; who with perversity in his heart devises evil continually, who spreads strife. Therefore his calamity will come suddenly; instantly he will be broken, and there will be no healing." (Proverbs 6:12-15, NASB)

"A wicked man shows a bold face, but as for the upright, he makes his way sure." (Proverbs 21:29, NASB)

Am I leading my siblings in disobedience?

"The righteous is a guide to his neighbor, but the way of the wicked leads them astray." (Proverbs 12:26, NASB)

"A little leaven leaveneth the whole lump." (Galatians 5:9)

"Looking diligently lest any man fail of the grace of God; lest any root of bitterness springing up trouble you, and thereby many be defiled." (Hebrews 12:15)

Do I disobey my parents when I am not with them?

"My son, keep thy father's commandment, and forsake not the law of thy mother: bind them continually upon thine heart, and tie them about thy neck. When thou goest, it shall lead thee; when thou sleepest, it shall keep thee; and when thou awakest, it shall talk with thee. For the commandment is a lamp; and the law is light; and reproofs of instruction are the way of life." (Proverbs 6:20-23)

"Therefore to him that knoweth to do good, and doeth it not, to him it is sin." (James 4:17)

Do I seek to deceive my parents with my words and actions, leading them to believe that I have obeyed when I have not?

"For there is nothing covered, that shall not be revealed; neither hid, that shall not be known. Therefore whatsoever ye have spoken in darkness shall be heard in the light; and that which ye have spoken in the ear in closets shall be proclaimed upon the housetops." (Luke 12:2-3)

"Put away from thee a froward mouth, and perverse lips put far from thee." (Proverbs 4:24)

Am I hiding areas of disobedience from my parents?

"O God, thou knowest my foolishness; and my sins are not hid from thee." (Psalm 69:5)

"For God shall bring every work into judgment, with every secret thing, whether it be good, or whether it be evil." (Ecclesiastes 12:14)

"He who conceals his transgressions will not prosper, but he who confesses and forsakes them will find compassion." (Proverbs 28:13, NASB)

Am I outwardly complying with my parents' commands while inwardly rebelling against them and God?

"Wherefore the Lord said, Forasmuch as this people draw near me with their mouth, and with their lips do honour me, but have removed their heart far from me, and their fear toward me is taught by the precept of men." (Isaiah 29:13)

"Like an earthen vessel overlaid with silver dross are burning lips and a wicked heart. He who hates disguises it with his lips, but he lays up deceit in his heart. When he speaks graciously, do not believe him, for there are seven abominations in his heart. Though his hatred covers itself with guile, his wickedness will be revealed before the assembly." (Proverbs 26:23-26, NASB)

"But the LORD said unto Samuel, Look not on his countenance, or on the height of his stature; because I have refused him: for the LORD seeth not as man seeth; for man looketh on the outward appearance, but the LORD looketh on the heart." (1 Samuel 16:7)

"Not with eyeservice, as menpleasers; but as the servants of Christ, doing the will of God from the heart; with good will doing service, as to the Lord, and not to men." (Ephesians 6:6-7)

Do I use my parents' sin or unlawful commands as an excuse for my own sin?

"Lay hands suddenly on no man, neither be partaker of other men's sins: keep thyself pure." (1 Timothy 5:22)

"And have no fellowship with the unfruitful works of darkness, but rather reprove them." (Ephesians 5:11)

"But he that doeth wrong shall receive for the wrong which he hath done: and there is no respect of persons." (Colossians 3:25)

"For God shall bring every work into judgment, with every secret thing, whether it be good, or whether it be evil." (Ecclesiastes 12:14)

If my parents have commanded me to do something that is truly sin against God, have I respectfully appealed to them?

"Then Peter and the other apostles answered and said, We ought to obey God rather than men." (Acts 5:29)

"And have no fellowship with the unfruitful works of darkness, but rather reprove them." (Ephesians 5:11)

"Moreover if thy brother shall trespass against thee, go and tell him his fault between thee and him alone: if he shall hear thee, thou hast gained thy brother." (Matthew 18:15)

If my parents have commanded me to do something that is truly sin, and they have rejected my appeals, have I sought the counsel of the authorities in my church?

"But if he will not hear thee, then take with thee one or two more, that in the mouth of two or three witnesses every word may be established. And if he shall neglect to hear them, tell it unto the church: but if he neglect to hear the church, let him be unto thee as an heathen man and a publican." (Matthew 18:16-17)

Do I see in my life the promised consequences for sinful rebellion against God and His delegated authorities?

"Because they rebelled against the words of God, and contemned the counsel of the most High: therefore he brought down their heart with labour; they fell down, and there was none to help. Then they cried unto the LORD in their trouble, and he saved them out of their distresses." (Psalm 107:11-13)

"Wherefore (as the Holy Ghost saith, To day if ye will hear his voice, harden not your hearts, as in the provocation, in the day of temptation in the wilderness: when your fathers tempted me, proved me, and saw my works forty years. Wherefore I was grieved with that generation, and said, They do alway err in their heart; and they have not known my ways. So I sware in my wrath, They shall not enter into my rest.)" (Hebrews 3:7-11)

"God setteth the solitary in families: he bringeth out those which are bound with chains: but the rebellious dwell in a dry land." (Psalm 68:6)

"I call heaven and earth to witness against you today, that I have set before you life and death, the blessing and the curse. So choose life in order that you may live, you and your descendants, by loving the LORD your God, by obeying His voice, and by holding fast to Him; for this is your life and the length of your days, that you may live in the land which the LORD swore to your fathers, to Abraham, Isaac, and Jacob, to give them." (Deuteronomy 30:19-20, NASB)

"The righteousness of the upright shall deliver them: but transgressors shall be taken in their own naughtiness." (Proverbs 11:6)

Do I continue to rebel because I do not recognize God's discipline for my rebellion?

"Be not deceived; God is not mocked: for whatsoever a man soweth, that shall he also reap. For he that soweth to his flesh shall of the flesh reap corruption; but he that soweth to the Spirit shall of the Spirit reap life everlasting." (Galatians 6:7-8)

"As righteousness tendeth to life: so he that pursueth evil pursueth it to his own death." (Proverbs 11:19)

"His own iniquities shall take the wicked himself, and he shall be holden with the cords of his sins." (Proverbs 5:22)

"He who sows iniquity will reap sorrow, and the rod of his anger will fail." (Proverbs 22:8, NKJV)

I sin against my parents through:

Rebellion against Their Lawful Corrections

Rebellion against God's correction and chastening, as it is administered through His representatives, is rebellion against God Himself. If I reject His loving discipline, I am a proud fool. I must listen to my parents as God speaks through them, guiding me in the way I should go. The only way I will grow in Christ is to acknowledge my sin, confess, repent, and change my attitudes and actions.

Am I refusing to acknowledge my parents' God-given responsibility to correct and discipline me?

"If ye endure chastening, God dealeth with you as with sons; for what son is he whom the father chasteneth not? But if ye be without chastisement, whereof all are partakers, then are ye bastards, and not sons. Furthermore we have had fathers of our flesh which corrected us, and we gave them reverence: shall we not much rather be in subjection unto the Father of spirits, and live?" (Hebrews 12:7-9)

"Correct thy son, and he shall give thee rest; yea, he shall give delight unto thy soul." (Proverbs 29:17)

"Train up a child in the way he should go: and when he is old, he will not depart from it." (Proverbs 22:6)

"Children, obey your parents in the Lord: for this is right. Honour thy father and mother; (which is the first commandment with promise;) that it may be well with thee, and thou mayest live long on the earth." (Ephesians 6:1-3)

Do I ignore or reject my parents' correction and discipline?

"He that turneth away his ear from hearing the law, even his prayer shall be abomination." (Proverbs 28:9)

"He is in the way of life that keepeth instruction: but he that refuseth reproof erreth." (Proverbs 10:17)

"A wise son heareth his father's instruction: but a scorner heareth not rebuke." (Proverbs 13:1)

"He that refuseth instruction despiseth his own soul: but he that heareth reproof getteth understanding." (Proverbs 15:32)

Do I become defensive when confronted with my sin?

"Every way of a man is right in his own eyes: but the LORD pondereth the hearts." (Proverbs 21:2)

"Who can understand his errors? cleanse thou me from secret faults." (Psalm 19:12)

"All the ways of a man are clean in his own eyes; but the LORD weigheth the spirits." (Proverbs 16:2)

"And he said unto them, Ye are they which justify yourselves before men; but God knoweth your hearts. . ." (Luke 16:15a)

When confronted with my sin, do I refuse to acknowledge my guilt? Do I make excuses for my sin, rather than accepting full responsibility for my words and actions?

"There is a generation that are pure in their own eyes, and yet is not washed from their filthiness." (Proverbs 30:12)

"The soul that sinneth, it shall die." (Ezekiel 18:20a)

Do I become angry or resentful when my parents or others attempt to help me see my errors and sin?

"He is in the way of life that keepeth instruction: but he that refuseth reproof erreth." (Proverbs 10:17)

"He that refuseth instruction despiseth his own soul: but he that heareth reproof getteth understanding." (Proverbs 15:32)

"A fool despiseth his father's instruction: but he that regardeth reproof is prudent." (Proverbs 15:5)

"Reprove not a scorner, lest he hate thee: rebuke a wise man, and he will love thee." (Proverbs 9:8)

"Correction is grievous unto him that forsaketh the way: and he that hateth reproof shall die." (Proverbs 15:10)

"Whoso loveth instruction loveth knowledge: but he that hateth reproof is brutish." (Proverbs 12:1)

Do I not take seriously those who seek to confront me with my sin?

"Fools make a mock at sin: but among the righteous there is favour." (Proverbs 14:9)

"Seest thou a man wise in his own conceit? there is more hope of a fool than of him." (Proverbs 26:12)

"If a wise man contendeth with a foolish man, whether he rage or laugh, there is no rest." (Proverbs 29:9)

Do I argue with my parents when they seek to correct me?

"A fool hath no delight in understanding, but that his heart may discover itself." (Proverbs 18:2)

"Strive not with a man without cause, if he have done thee no harm." (Proverbs 3:30)

"Keeping away from strife is an honor for a man, but any fool will quarrel." (Proverbs 20:3, NASB)

"A fool's lips enter into contention, and his mouth calleth for strokes." (Proverbs 18:6)

Do I try to deny or hide my sin? Am I unwilling to trust the insights and reproofs of others?

"He that covereth his sins shall not prosper: but whoso confesseth and forsaketh them shall have mercy. Happy is the man that feareth alway: but he that hardeneth his heart shall fall into mischief." (Proverbs 28:13-14)

"O God, thou knowest my foolishness; and my sins are not hid from thee." (Psalm 69:5)

"The heart is deceitful above all things, and desperately wicked: who can know it?" (Jeremiah 17:9)

"Be not wise in thine own eyes: fear the LORD, and depart from evil." (Proverbs 3:7)

Do I seek to cast blame on my parents or others for my own sins?

"Because it is written, Be ye holy; for I am holy. And if ye call on the Father, who without respect of persons judgeth according to every man's work, pass the time of your sojourning here in fear." (1 Peter 1:16-17)

"And he said unto them, Ye are they which justify yourselves before men; but God knoweth your hearts. . ." (Luke 16:15a)

"But every man is tempted, when he is drawn away of his own lust, and enticed. Then when lust hath conceived, it bringeth forth sin: and sin, when it is finished, bringeth forth death." (James 1:14-15)

Do I refuse to acknowledge my sin as sin?

"There is a generation that are pure in their own eyes, and yet is not washed from their filthiness." (Proverbs 30:12)

"A servant will not be corrected by words: for though he understand he will not answer." (Proverbs 29:19)

"If we say that we have no sin, we deceive ourselves, and the truth is not in us. If we confess our sins, he is faithful and just to forgive us our sins, and to cleanse us from all unrighteousness. If we say that we have not sinned, we make him a liar, and his word is not in us." (1 John 1:8-10)

Do I think my parents are too strict or particular about my attitudes and actions?

"Be not wise in thine own eyes: fear the LORD, and depart from evil." (Proverbs 3:7)

"The heart is deceitful above all things, and desperately wicked: who can know it?" (Jeremiah 17:9)

"For whosoever shall keep the whole law, and yet offend in one point, he is guilty of all." (James 2:10)

"And ye have forgotten the exhortation which speaketh unto you as unto children, My son, despise not thou the chastening of the Lord, nor faint when thou art rebuked of him: for whom the Lord loveth he chasteneth, and scourgeth every son whom he receiveth." (Hebrews 12:5-6)

Do I complain about the disciplines that my parents lovingly impose on me?

"Wherefore doth a living man complain, a man for the punishment of his sins?" (Lamentations 3:39)

"Behold, happy is the man whom God correcteth: therefore despise not thou the chastening of the Almighty." (Job 5:17)

"My son, despise not the chastening of the LORD; neither be weary of his correction: for whom the LORD loveth he correcteth; even as a father the son in whom he delighteth." (Proverbs 3:11-12)

"Now no chastening for the present seemeth to be joyous, but grievous: nevertheless afterward it yieldeth the peaceable fruit of righteousness unto them which are exercised thereby." (Hebrews 12:11)

Do I avoid associating with my parents and others that might confront me with my sin?

"For every one that doeth evil hateth the light, neither cometh to the light, lest his deeds should be reproved." (John 3:20)

"A scorner loveth not one that reproveth him: neither will he go unto the wise." (Proverbs 15:12)

Is my relationship with my parents healthy and pleasant, or is it filled with strife and bitterness?

"Behold, how good and how pleasant it is for brethren to dwell together in unity!" (Psalm 133:1)

"Only by pride cometh contention: but with the well advised is wisdom." (Proverbs 13:10)

"Looking diligently lest any man fail of the grace of God; lest any root of bitterness springing up trouble you, and thereby many be defiled; lest there be any fornicator, or profane person, as Esau, who for one morsel of meat sold his birthright. For ye know how that afterward, when he would have inherited the blessing, he was rejected: for he found no place of repentance, though he sought it carefully with tears." (Hebrews 12:15-17)

Am I seeking the companionship of those who will approve of my sinful attitudes and actions?

"It is better to hear the rebuke of the wise, than for a man to hear the song of fools." (Ecclesiastes 7:5)

"The heart of him that hath understanding seeketh knowledge: but the mouth of fools feedeth on foolishness." (Proverbs15:14)

"He that saith unto the wicked, Thou are righteous; him shall the people curse, nations shall abhor him: but to them that rebuke him shall be delight, and a good blessing shall come upon them." (Proverbs 24:24-25)

Am I unwilling to discontinue friendships and associations that encourage my rebellious attitude?

"Blessed is the man that walketh not in the counsel of the ungodly, nor standeth in the way of sinners, nor sitteth in the seat of the scornful." (Psalm 1:1)

"Do not be deceived: 'Bad company corrupts good morals.'" (1 Corinthians 15:33, NASB)

Do I refuse to acknowledge and repent of my wrongs even after being disciplined for them?

"The desire accomplished is sweet to the soul: but it is abomination to fools to depart from evil." (Proverbs 13:19)

"He, that being often reproved hardeneth his neck, shall suddenly be destroyed, and that without remedy." (Proverbs 29:1)

"Poverty and shame shall be to him that refuseth instruction: but he that regardeth reproof shall be honoured." (Proverbs 13:18)

"A reproof entereth more into a wise man than an hundred stripes into a fool." (Proverbs 17:10)

Do I seek to pacify those who correct me without truly repenting of my sin?

"For thou desirest not sacrifice; else would I give it: thou delightest not in burnt offering. The sacrifices of God are a broken spirit: a broken and a contrite heart, O God, thou wilt not despise." (Psalm 51:16-17)

"...for the LORD seeth not as man seeth; for man looketh on the outward appearance, but the LORD looketh on the heart." (1 Samuel 16:7b)

"Then the Lord said to him, 'Now you Pharisees make the outside of the cup and dish clean, but your inward part is full of greed and wickedness.'" (Luke 11:39, NKJV)

"And they come unto thee as the people cometh, and they sit before thee as my people, and they hear thy words, but they will not do them: for with their mouth they shew much love, but their heart goeth after their covetousness. And, lo, thou art unto them as a very lovely song of one that hath a pleasant voice, and can play well on an instrument: for they hear thy words, but they do them not." (Ezekiel 33:31-32)

Do I verbally acknowledge my sin, but continue to engage in it without any outward signs of true repentance?

"As a dog returneth to his vomit, so a fool returneth to his folly." (Proverbs 26:11)

"But be ye doers of the word, and not hearers only, deceiving your own selves. For if any be a hearer of the word, and not a doer, he is like unto a man beholding his natural face in a glass: for he beholdeth himself, and goeth his way, and straightway forgetteth what manner of man he was." (James 1:22-24)

When confronted with my sin, do I refuse to repent? Do I not care, even when I know I am sinning?

"And even as they did not like to retain God in their knowledge, God gave them over to a reprobate mind, to do those things which are not convenient; being filled with all unrighteousness, fornication, wickedness, covetousness, maliciousness; full of envy, murder, debate, deceit, malignity; whisperers, backbiters, haters of God, despiteful, proud, boasters, inventors of evil things, disobedient to parents, without understanding, covenantbreakers, without natural affection, implacable, unmerciful: who knowing the judgment of God, that they which commit such things are worthy of death, not only do the same, but have pleasure in them that do them." (Romans 1:28-32)

"Because I have called, and ye refused; I have stretched out my hand, and no man regarded; but ye have set at nought all my counsel, and would none of my reproof: I also will laugh at your calamity; I will mock when your fear cometh; When your fear cometh as desolation, and your destruction cometh as a whirlwind; when distress and anguish cometh upon you. Then shall they call upon me, but I will not answer; they shall seek me early, but they shall not find me: for that they hated knowledge, and did not choose the fear of the LORD: they would none of my counsel: they despised all my reproof." (Proverbs 1:24-30)

When God graciously brings conviction to me through His Holy Spirit, do I continue in my rebellion by refusing to repent?

"If ye will fear the LORD, and serve him, and obey his voice, and not rebel against the commandment of the LORD, then shall both ye and also the king that reigneth over you continue following the LORD your God: but if ye will not obey the voice of the LORD, but rebel against the commandment of the LORD, then shall the hand of the LORD be against you, as it was against your fathers. Now therefore stand and see this great thing, which the LORD will do before your eyes." (1 Samuel 12:14-16)

"Or despisest thou the riches of his goodness and forbearance and longsuffering; not knowing that the goodness of God leadeth thee to repentance? But after thy hardness and impenitent heart treasurest up unto thyself wrath against the day of wrath and revelation of the righteous judgment of God; who will render to every man according to his deeds." (Romans 2:4-6)

"It is a fearful thing to fall into the hands of the living God." (Hebrews 10:31)

Do I refuse to believe that stubbornness and rebellion will bring pain and discipline into my life?

"Be not deceived; God is not mocked: for whatsoever a man soweth, that shall he also reap." (Galatians 6:7)

"He is wise in heart, and mighty in strength: who hath hardened himself against him, and hath prospered?" (Job 9:4)

"He, that being often reproved hardeneth his neck, shall suddenly be destroyed, and that without remedy." (Proverbs 29:1)

"Wherefore (as the Holy Ghost saith, To day if ye will hear his voice, Harden not your hearts, as in the provocation, in the day of temptation in the wilderness: when your fathers tempted me, proved me, and saw my works forty years. Wherefore I was grieved with that generation, and said, They do alway err in their heart; and they have not known my ways. So I sware in my wrath, They shall not enter into my rest.)" (Hebrews 3:7-11)

Do I sense a loss of fellowship with God?

"Behold, the LORD's hand is not shortened, that it cannot save; neither his ear heavy, that it cannot hear: but your iniquities have separated between you and your God, and your sins have hid his face from you, that he will not hear." (Isaiah 59:1-2)

"So I gave them up unto their own hearts' lust: and they walked in their own counsels." (Psalm 81:12)

"And he said, Go, and tell this people, Hear ye indeed, but understand not; and see ye indeed, but perceive not. Make the heart of this people fat, and make their ears heavy, and shut their eyes; lest they see with their eyes, and hear with their ears, and understand with their heart, and convert, and be healed." (Isaiah 6:9-10)

"For rebellion is as the sin of witchcraft, and stubbornness is as iniquity and idolatry. Because thou hast rejected the word of the LORD, he hath also rejected thee from being king." (1 Samuel 15:23)

Do I feel like God is not hearing me when I pray?

"A scorner seeketh wisdom, and findeth it not: but knowledge is easy unto him that understandeth." (Proverbs 14:6)

"But they refused to hearken, and pulled away the shoulder, and stopped their ears, that they should not hear. Yea, they made their hearts as an adamant stone, lest they should hear the law, and the words which the LORD of hosts hath sent in his spirit by the former prophets: therefore came a great wrath from the LORD of hosts. Therefore it is come to pass, that as he cried, and they would not hear; so they cried, and I would not hear, saith the LORD of hosts." (Zechariah 7:11-13)

Am I suffering consequences that are due to my own foolish decisions and rebellion?

"It is a fearful thing to fall into the hands of the living God." (Hebrews 10:31)

"Because they rebelled against the words of God, and contemned the counsel of the most High: therefore he brought down their heart with labour; they fell down, and there was none to help." (Psalm 107:11-12)

"His own iniquities shall take the wicked himself, and he shall be holden with the cords of his sins." (Proverbs 5:22)

"If ye be willing and obedient, ye shall eat the good of the land: but if ye refuse and rebel, ye shall be devoured with the sword: for the mouth of the LORD hath spoken it." (Isaiah 1:19-20)

"Stern discipline is for him who forsakes the way; he who hates reproof will die." (Proverbs 15:10, NASB)

I sin against my parents through:

Cursing

I must not wish evil on my parents. To dwell on perceived offenses, imagining revenge, and meditating on my anger and bitterness, is to sin against God and my parents. To wish evil on God's delegated authorities is to rebel against His sovereign, loving will in my life.

Do I, in pride, imagine or wish evil on my parents?

"How long will ye imagine mischief against a man? ye shall be slain all of you: as a bowing wall shall ye be, and as a tottering fence. They only consult to cast him down from his excellency: they delight in lies: they bless with their mouth, but they curse inwardly." (Psalm 62:3-4)

"And let none of you imagine evil in your hearts against his neighbour; and love no false oath: for all these are things that I hate, saith the LORD." (Zechariah 8:17)

"And he said unto his men, The LORD forbid that I should do this thing unto my master, the LORD's anointed, to stretch forth mine hand against him, seeing he is the anointed of the LORD." (1 Samuel 24:6)

"He that wasteth his father, and chaseth away his mother, is a son that causeth shame, and bringeth reproach." (Proverbs 19:26)

Have I had thoughts of hatred or expressed feelings of anger and hatred for my parents?

"Let all bitterness, and wrath, and anger, and clamour, and evil speaking, be put away from you, with all malice." (Ephesians 4:31)

"Curse not the king, no not in thy thought; and curse not the rich in thy bedchamber: for a bird of the air shall carry the voice, and that which hath wings shall tell the matter." (Ecclesiastes 10:20)

"He that saith he is in the light, and hateth his brother, is in darkness even until now. He that loveth his brother abideth in the light, and there is none occasion of stumbling in him. But he that hateth his brother is in darkness, and walketh in darkness, and knoweth not whither he goeth, because that darkness hath blinded his eyes." (1 John 2:9-11)

"Thou shalt not revile the gods, nor curse the ruler of thy people." (Exodus 22:28)

Have I spoken cruel words to my parents that need to be confessed?

"But now ye also put off all these; anger, wrath, malice, blasphemy, filthy communication out of your mouth." (Colossians 3:8)

"For even hereunto were ye called: because Christ also suffered for us, leaving us an example, that ye should follow his steps: Who did no sin, neither was guile found in his mouth." (1 Peter 2:21-22)

"For by thy words thou shalt be justified, and by thy words thou shalt be condemned." (Matthew 12:37)

Do I desire to see my parents suffer for wrongs they have allegedly committed against me?

"For we know him that hath said, Vengeance belongeth unto me, I will recompense, saith the Lord. And again, The Lord shall judge his people. It is a fearful thing to fall into the hands of the living God." (Hebrews 10:30-31)

"Recompense to no man evil for evil. Provide things honest in the sight of all men. If it be possible, as much as lieth in you, live peaceably with all men. Dearly beloved, avenge not yourselves, but rather give place unto wrath: for it is written, Vengeance is mine; I will repay, saith the Lord. Therefore if thine enemy hunger, feed him; if he thirst, give him drink: for in so doing thou shalt heap coals of fire on his head. Be not overcome of evil, but overcome evil with good." (Romans 12:17-21)

"Not rendering evil for evil, or railing for railing: but contrariwise blessing; knowing that ye are thereunto called, that ye should inherit a blessing." (1 Peter 3:9)

"Bless them which persecute you: bless, and curse not." (Romans 12:14)

Do I delight in seeing my parents go through times of testing, suffering, or failure?

"Rejoice not when thine enemy falleth, and let not thine heart be glad when he stumbleth: Lest the LORD see it, and it displease him, and he turn away his wrath from him." (Proverbs 24:17-18)

"[Charity] rejoiceth not in iniquity, but rejoiceth in the truth." (1 Corinthians 13:6)

"Whoso mocketh the poor reproacheth his Maker: and he that is glad at calamities shall not be unpunished." (Proverbs 17:5)

Am I demonstrating my rebellion against God by bitterly cursing the parents He has placed over me?

"Thou shalt not revile the gods, nor curse the ruler of thy people." (Exodus 22:28)

"Their throat is an open sepulchre; with their tongues they have used deceit; the poison of asps is under their lips: Whose mouth is full of cursing and bitterness: Their feet are swift to shed blood: destruction and misery are in their ways: and the way of peace have they not known: there is no fear of God before their eyes." (Romans 3:13-18)

"The wicked, through the pride of his countenance, will not seek after God: God is not in all his thoughts. His ways are always grievous; thy judgments are far above out of his sight: as for all his enemies, he puffeth at them. He hath said in his heart, I shall not be moved: for I shall never be in adversity. His mouth is full of cursing and deceit and fraud: under his tongue is mischief and vanity." (Psalm 10:4-7)

Am I claiming to love and obey God while speaking words of hatred and vengeance to my parents?

"There is a generation that curseth their father, and doth not bless their mother. There is a generation that are pure in their own eyes, and yet is not washed from their filthiness. There is a generation, O how lofty are their eyes! and their eyelids are lifted up." (Proverbs 30:11-13)

"If any man among you seem to be religious, and bridleth not his tongue, but deceiveth his own heart, this man's religion is vain." (James 1:26)

"But the tongue can no man tame; it is an unruly evil, full of deadly poison. Therewith bless we God, even the Father; and therewith curse we men, which are made after the similitude of God. Out of the same mouth proceedeth blessing and cursing. My brethren, these things ought not so to be. Doth a fountain send forth at the same place sweet water and bitter? Can the fig tree, my brethren, bear olive berries? either a vine, figs? so can no fountain both yield salt water and fresh." (James 3:8-12)

". . .for out of the abundance of the heart the mouth speaketh. A good man out of the good treasure of the heart bringeth forth good things: and an evil man out of the evil treasure bringeth forth evil things." (Matthew 12:34b-35)

Am I willing to accept the consequences God promises for those who curse the authorities God has placed over them?

"For every one that curseth his father or his mother shall be surely put to death: he hath cursed his father or his mother; his blood shall be upon him." (Leviticus 20:9)

"Whoso curseth his father or his mother, his lamp shall be put out in obscure darkness." (Proverbs 20:20)

"As he loved cursing, so let it come unto him: as he delighted not in blessing, so let it be far from him. As he clothed himself with cursing like as with his garment, so let it come into his bowels like water, and like oil into his bones." (Psalm 109:17-18)

"Whoso diggeth a pit shall fall therein: and he that rolleth a stone, it will return upon him." (Proverbs 26:27)

"But God shall shoot at them with an arrow; suddenly shall they be wounded. So they shall make their own tongue to fall upon themselves: all that see them shall flee away." (Psalm 64:7-8)

"Thou lovest all devouring words, O thou deceitful tongue. God shall likewise destroy thee for ever, he shall take thee away, and pluck thee out of thy dwelling place, and root thee out of the land of the living." (Psalm 52:4-5)

I sin against my parents through:

Mocking

A true and godly respect for my parents will not tolerate an attitude of proud mockery. My parents must always be viewed with reverence and honor, and I will refuse to mimic or ridicule them with my words or my actions.

Do I laugh at, scorn, or make light of my parents and their beliefs, ideas, and actions?

"A scorner loveth not one that reproveth him: neither will he go unto the wise." (Proverbs 15:12)

"If any man among you seem to be religious, and bridleth not his tongue, but deceiveth his own heart, this man's religion is vain." (James 1:26)

Do I make my parents look like fools in front of others?

"How long, ye simple ones, will ye love simplicity? and the scorners delight in their scorning, and fools hate knowledge? . . . I also will laugh at your calamity; I will mock when your fear cometh." (Proverbs 1:22 and 26)

Do I delight in making fun of my parents and their ideas?

"How long, ye simple ones, will ye love simplicity? and the scorners delight in their scorning, and fools hate knowledge? Turn you at my reproof: behold, I will pour out my spirit unto you, I will make known my words unto you." (Proverbs 1:22-23)

"It is as sport to a fool to do mischief: but a man of understanding hath wisdom." (Proverbs 10:23)

Do I imitate my parents or quote their words in angry or disrespectful ways?

"Proud and haughty scorner is his name, who dealeth in proud wrath." (Proverbs 21:24)

"But they mocked the messengers of God, and despised his words, and misused his prophets, until the wrath of the LORD arose against his people, till there was no remedy." (2 Chronicles 36:16)

Do I laugh at my parents' attempts to counsel and correct me?

"Fools make a mock at sin: but among the righteous there is favour." (Proverbs 14:9)

"If a wise man contendeth with a foolish man, whether he rage or laugh, there is no rest." (Proverbs 29:9)

"For as the crackling of thorns under a pot, so is the laughter of the fool: this also is vanity." (Ecclesiastes 7:6)

Do I join with my siblings or friends when they mock or show disrespect to my parents?

"The eye that mocketh at his father, and despiseth to obey his mother, the ravens of the valley shall pick it out, and the young eagles shall eat it." (Proverbs 30:17)

"Honour thy father and thy mother: that thy days may be long upon the land which the LORD thy God giveth thee." (Exodus 20:12)

"Because sentence against an evil work is not executed speedily, therefore the heart of the sons of men is fully set in them to do evil." (Ecclesiastes 8:11)

Do I, in response to my parents, exchange mocking facial expressions, gestures, etc. with my siblings or friends?

"Blessed is the man that walketh not in the counsel of the ungodly, nor standeth in the way of sinners, nor sitteth in the seat of the scornful. But his delight is in the law of the LORD; and in his law doth he meditate day and night." (Psalm 1:1-2)

"Against whom do ye sport yourselves? against whom make ye a wide mouth, and draw out the tongue? are ye not children of transgression, a seed of falsehood?" (Isaiah 57:4)

"The shew of their countenance doth witness against them; and they declare their sin as Sodom, they hide it not. Woe unto their soul! for they have rewarded evil unto themselves." (Isaiah 3:9)

"Every one that is proud in heart is an abomination to the LORD: though hand join in hand, he shall not be unpunished." (Proverbs 16:5)

"A naughty person, a wicked man, walketh with a froward mouth. He winketh with his eyes, he speaketh with his feet, he teacheth with his fingers; frowardness is in his heart, he deviseth mischief continually; he soweth discord. Therefore shall his calamity come suddenly; suddenly shall he be broken without remedy." (Proverbs 6:12-15)

Is my mockery destroying my relationship with my parents?

"The thought of foolishness is sin: and the scorner is an abomination to men." (Proverbs 24:9)

"If a wise man contendeth with a foolish man, whether he rage or laugh, there is no rest." (Proverbs 29:9)

"A wholesome tongue is a tree of life: but perverseness therein is a breach in the spirit." (Proverbs 15:4)

Is my whole family suffering under my scornful attitude?

"Scoffers set a city aflame, but wise men turn away wrath." (Proverbs 29:8, NKJV)

"Cast out the scorner, and contention shall go out; yea, strife and reproach shall cease." (Proverbs 22:10)

"He that troubleth his own house shall inherit the wind: and the fool shall be servant to the wise of heart." (Proverbs 11:29)

Am I willing to accept the consequences God promises for scorners?

"The eye that mocketh at his father, and despiseth to obey his mother, the ravens of the valley shall pick it out, and the young eagles shall eat it." (Proverbs 30:17)

"Surely he scorneth the scorners: but he giveth grace unto the lowly." (Proverbs 3:34)

"Judgments are prepared for scorners, and stripes for the back of fools." (Proverbs 19:29)

"If thou be wise, thou shalt be wise for thyself: but if thou scornest, thou alone shalt bear it." (Proverbs 9:12)

I sin against my parents through:

Refractory and Scandalous Carriage that Proves a Shame and Dishonor to Them and Their Government

Obstinate, sullen disobedience has no place in my life if I am going to show my parents the respect that God requires of me. To stubbornly refuse to obey is the manifestation of a hard and rebellious heart against God. As He has promised, God will discipline me for my rebellion. My selfish behavior will bring sorrow and shame to my family. God calls me to humble repentance.

Do I openly ignore or resist my parents' efforts to lead me?

"For rebellion is as the sin of witchcraft, and stubbornness is as iniquity and idolatry. Because thou hast rejected the word of the LORD, he hath also rejected thee from being king." (1 Samuel 15:23)

"But they obeyed not, neither inclined their ear, but made their neck stiff, that they might not hear, nor receive instruction." (Jeremiah 17:23)

Do I refuse to follow or cooperate with my parents as they lead our family?

"Be ye not as the horse, or as the mule, which have no understanding. . ."(Psalm 32:9a)

"A wicked man hardeneth his face: but as for the upright, he directeth his way." (Proverbs 21:29)

"But they refused to hearken, and pulled away the shoulder, and stopped their ears, that they should not hear." (Zechariah 7:11)

Do I knowingly, and even spitefully, go against my parents' wishes and standards?

"The integrity of the upright shall guide them: but the perverseness of transgressors shall destroy them." (Proverbs 11:3)

"Whoso keepeth the law is a wise son: but he that is a companion of riotous men shameth his father." (Proverbs 28:7)

"An evil man seeketh only rebellion: therefore a cruel messenger shall be sent against him." (Proverbs 17:11)

"Therefore to him that knoweth to do good, and doeth it not, to him it is sin." (James 4:17)

Do I say, do, or wear things in public that shame my parents?

"Wise men lay up knowledge: but the mouth of the foolish is near destruction." (Proverbs 10:14)

"The words of a wise man's mouth are gracious; but the lips of a fool will swallow up himself." (Ecclesiastes 10:12)

"A virtuous woman is a crown to her husband: but she that maketh ashamed is as rottenness in his bones." (Proverbs 12:4)

"Whoso keepeth the law is a wise son: but he that is a companion of riotous men shameth his father." (Proverbs 28:7)

Do I refuse to yield to my parents when I disagree with them?

"Woe unto them that are wise in their own eyes, and prudent in their own sight!" (Isaiah 5:21)

"Seest thou a man wise in his own conceit? there is more hope of a fool than of him." (Proverbs 26:12)

"Let nothing be done through strife or vainglory; but in lowliness of mind let each esteem other better than themselves." (Philippians 2:3)

"Proud and haughty scorner is his name, who dealeth in proud wrath." (Proverbs 21:24)

"Be kindly affectioned one to another with brotherly love; in honour preferring one another." (Romans 12:10)

Am I unwilling to yield to my parents, even when I know they are right?

"He that covereth his sins shall not prosper: but whoso confesseth and forsaketh them shall have mercy. Happy is the man that feareth alway: but he that hardeneth his heart shall fall into mischief." (Proverbs 28:13-14)

"I also will choose their delusions, and will bring their fears upon them; because when I called, none did answer; when I spake, they did not hear: but they did evil before mine eyes, and chose that in which I delighted not." (Isaiah 66:4)

"But they hearkened not, nor inclined their ear, but walked in the counsels and in the imagination of their evil heart, and went backward, and not forward." (Jeremiah 7:24)

"He, that being often reproved hardeneth his neck, shall suddenly be destroyed, and that without remedy." (Proverbs 29:1)

Has my selfishness, laziness, and negligence brought public shame and dishonor to my parents and our family?

"He that gathereth in summer is a wise son: but he that sleepeth in harvest is a son that causeth shame." (Proverbs 10:5)

"I went by the field of the slothful, and by the vineyard of the man void of understanding; and, lo, it was all grown over with thorns, and nettles had covered the face thereof, and the stone wall thereof was broken down." (Proverbs 24:30-31)

"A wise son maketh a glad father: but a foolish son is the heaviness of his mother." (Proverbs 10:1b)

"He that wasteth his father, and chaseth away his mother, is a son that causeth shame, and bringeth reproach." (Proverbs 19:26)

Have my shameful attitudes and actions hindered my father in his responsibilities and goals?

"They were all ashamed of a people that could not profit them, nor be an help nor profit, but a shame, and also a reproach." (Isaiah 30:5)

"A foolish son is the calamity of his father: and the contentions of a wife are a continual dropping." (Proverbs 19:13)

Has my stubbornness and shameful behavior harmed my relationship with my parents?

"The king's favour is toward a wise servant: but his wrath is against him that causeth shame." (Proverbs 14:35)

"A foolish son is a grief to his father, and bitterness to her that bare him." (Proverbs 17:25)

Has my pride brought shame, disappointment, and embarrassment to my parents?

"When pride cometh, then cometh shame: but with the lowly is wisdom." (Proverbs 11:2)

"He that wasteth his father, and chaseth away his mother, is a son that causeth shame, and bringeth reproach." (Proverbs 19:26)

"The king's favour is toward a wise servant: but his wrath is against him that causeth shame." (Proverbs 14:35)

"He that begetteth a fool doeth it to his sorrow: and the father of a fool hath no joy." (Proverbs 17:21)

"These six things doth the LORD hate: yea, seven are an abomination unto him: a proud look, a lying tongue, and hands that shed innocent blood, an heart that deviseth wicked imaginations, feet that be swift in running to mischief, a false witness that speaketh lies, and he that soweth discord among brethren." (Proverbs 6:16-19)

Has shame come to our household as a result of my refusal to accept the instruction of God's Word and His leading as directed through my parents?

"Poverty and shame shall be to him that refuseth instruction: but he that regardeth reproof shall be honoured." (Proverbs 13:18)

"O LORD, are not thine eyes upon the truth? thou hast stricken them, but they have not grieved; thou hast consumed them, but they have refused to receive correction: they have made their faces harder than a rock; they have refused to return." (Jeremiah 5:3)

"Righteousness exalteth a nation: but sin is a reproach to any people." (Proverbs 14:34)

"He that troubleth his own house shall inherit the wind: and the fool shall be servant to the wise of heart." (Proverbs 11:29)

Have my actions brought dishonor to God's name?

"Whom hast thou reproached and blasphemed? and against whom hast thou exalted thy voice, and lifted up thine eyes on high? even against the Holy One of Israel." (Isaiah 37:23)

"Let as many servants as are under the yoke count their own masters worthy of all honour, that the name of God and his doctrine be not blasphemed." (1 Timothy 6:1)

"To be discreet, chaste, keepers at home, good, obedient to their own husbands, that the word of God be not blasphemed." (Titus 2:5)

"Woe unto them! for they have fled from me: destruction unto them! because they have transgressed against me: though I have redeemed them, yet they have spoken lies against me." (Hosea 7:13)

Do I recognize my sin and rebellion and am I willing to humble myself, confess my sin to God and to my parents, and repent?

"For thou desirest not sacrifice; else would I give it: thou delightest not in burnt offering. The sacrifices of God are a broken spirit: a broken and a contrite heart, O God, thou wilt not despise." (Psalm 51:16-17)

"Wherefore lay apart all filthiness and superfluity of naughtiness, and receive with meekness the engrafted word, which is able to save your souls. But be ye doers of the word, and not hearers only, deceiving your own selves." (James 1:21-22)

"Confess your faults one to another, and pray one for another, that ye may be healed. The effectual fervent prayer of a righteous man availeth much." (James 5:16)

"Depart from evil, and do good; seek peace, and pursue it." (Psalm 34:14)

My relationship with God and my parents can be restored through:

Confession and Repentance of My Sin

Sin separates us from God. Without faith in Christ's death and resurrection, we are separated from God forever. We cannot please Him. When we place our faith in Jesus as our only means of satisfying God's righteous requirements, we are clothed in Christ's righteousness and our sins are covered. Because of Christ, we are restored to fellowship with God and given the Holy Spirit who enables us to obey God.

But, until heaven, we will still struggle with our old sin nature that desires to disobey. Galatians 5:17 says, "For the flesh lusteth against the Spirit, and the Spirit against the flesh: and these are contrary the one to the other: so that ye cannot do the things that ye would." We will still sin, but Jesus is our mediator, sitting at the right hand of God the Father, interceding for us. Because we are in Christ, we can approach the Father and ask forgiveness for our sins, and we are assured that He will forgive us. We are no longer in bondage to sin.

No matter what mistakes we have made, or how far we have wandered from Him, God will welcome us back when we repent. Like the prodigal son, if you have rebelled against God or against your parents, you can face your sin, turn from it, confess it, and ask forgiveness. God will give you the strength and the grace to start again.

Do I believe that, because I was born a sinner, I am eternally separated from God, apart from saving faith in Jesus Christ?

"For all have sinned, and come short of the glory of God; being justified freely by his grace through the redemption that is in Christ Jesus." (Romans 3:23-24)

"Wherefore, as by one man sin entered into the world, and death by sin; and so death passed upon all men, for that all have sinned." (Romans 5:12)

"For the wages of sin is death; but the gift of God is eternal life through Jesus Christ our Lord." (Romans 6:23)

Have I placed my faith in the saving work of Jesus on the cross? Do I believe that His sinless life, death, and resurrection are my only means of right relationship with God?

"Jesus saith unto him, I am the way, the truth, and the life: no man cometh unto the Father, but by me." (John 14:6)

"And you hath he quickened, who were dead in trespasses and sins; wherein in time past ye walked according to the course of this world, according to the prince of the power of the air, the spirit that now worketh in the children of disobedience: among whom also we all had our conversation in times past in the lusts of our flesh, fulfilling the desires of the flesh and of the mind; and were by nature the children of wrath, even as others. But God, who is rich in mercy, for his great love wherewith he loved us, even when we were dead in sins, hath quickened us together with Christ, (by grace ye are saved;) and hath raised us up together, and made us sit together in heavenly places in Christ Jesus: that in the ages to come he might shew the exceeding riches of his grace in his kindness toward us through Christ Jesus. For by grace are ye saved through faith; and that not of yourselves: it is the gift of God: not of works, lest any man should boast. For we are his workmanship, created in Christ Jesus unto good works, which God hath before ordained that we should walk in them." (Ephesians 2:1-10)

"My little children, these things write I unto you, that ye sin not. And if any man sin, we have an advocate with the Father, Jesus Christ the righteous: and he is the propitiation for our sins: and not for ours only, but also for the sins of the whole world." (1 John 2:1-2)

"For there is one God, and one mediator between God and men, the man Christ Jesus." (1 Timothy 2:5)

"Because the carnal mind is enmity against God: for it is not subject to the law of God, neither indeed can be. So then they that are in the flesh cannot please God." (Romans 8:7-8)

Do I believe that as a believer, saved by grace, I am no longer in bondage to sin and my sinful desires?

"Therefore if any man be in Christ, he is a new creature: old things are passed away; behold, all things are become new." (2 Corinthians 5:17)

"Therefore, brethren, we are debtors, not to the flesh, to live after the flesh. For if ye live after the flesh, ye shall die: but if ye through the Spirit do mortify the deeds of the body, ye shall live. For as many as are led by the Spirit of God, they are the sons of God. For ye have not received the spirit of bondage again to fear; but ye have received the Spirit of adoption, whereby we cry, Abba, Father." (Romans 8:12-15)

Have I been in rebellion against God?

"But they and our fathers dealt proudly, and hardened their necks, and hearkened not to thy commandments, and refused to obey, neither were mindful of thy wonders that thou didst among them; but hardened their necks, and in their rebellion appointed a captain to return to their bondage: but thou art a God ready to pardon, gracious and merciful, slow to anger, and of great kindness, and forsookest them not." (Nehemiah 9:16-17)

"For if ye turn again unto the LORD, your brethren and your children shall find compassion before them that lead them captive, so that they shall come again into this land: for the LORD your God is gracious and merciful, and will not turn away his face from you, if ye return unto him." (2 Chronicles 30:9)

"Against thee, thee only, have I sinned, and done this evil in thy sight. . ." (Psalm 51:4a)

"Draw nigh to God, and he will draw nigh to you. Cleanse your hands, ye sinners; and purify your hearts, ye double minded." (James 4:8)

Am I recognizing God's call to repentance in my life?

"For God maketh my heart soft, and the Almighty troubleth me." (Job 23:16)

"And I will give them an heart to know me, that I am the LORD: and they shall be my people, and I will be their God: for they shall return unto me with their whole heart." (Jeremiah 24:7)

"For he is our God; and we are the people of his pasture, and the sheep of his hand. To day if ye will hear his voice, harden not your heart, as in the provocation, and as in the day of temptation in the wilderness." (Psalm 95:7-8)

Am I praying for a humble and repentant heart?

"A new heart also will I give you, and a new spirit will I put within you: and I will take away the stony heart out of your flesh, and I will give you an heart of flesh." (Ezekiel 36:26)

"And I will give them one heart, and I will put a new spirit within you; and I will take the stony heart out of their flesh, and will give them an heart of flesh: that they may walk in my statutes, and keep mine ordinances, and do them: and they shall be my people, and I will be their God. But as for them whose heart walketh after the heart of their detestable things and their abominations, I will recompense their way upon their own heads, saith the Lord GOD." (Ezekiel 11:19-21)

Am I willing to acknowledge my sin?

"Wash me throughly from mine iniquity, and cleanse me from my sin. For I acknowledge my transgressions: and my sin is ever before me." (Psalm 51:2-3)

"He that covereth his sins shall not prosper: but whoso confesseth and forsaketh them shall have mercy." (Proverbs 28:13)

Is my heart humbled and broken before God as I recognize my sin against Him?

"Be afflicted, and mourn, and weep: let your laughter be turned to mourning, and your joy to heaviness. Humble yourselves in the sight of the Lord, and he shall lift you up." (James 4:9-10)

"The LORD is nigh unto them that are of a broken heart; and saveth such as be of a contrite spirit." (Psalm 34:18)

"The sacrifices of God are a broken spirit: a broken and a contrite heart, O God, thou wilt not despise." (Psalm 51:17)

"Therefore also now, saith the LORD, turn ye even to me with all your heart, and with fasting, and with weeping, and with mourning: and rend your heart, and not your garments, and turn unto the LORD your God: for he is gracious and merciful, slow to anger, and of great kindness, and repenteth him of the evil. Who knoweth if he will return and repent, and leave a blessing behind him; even a meat offering and a drink offering unto the LORD your God?" (Joel 2:12-14)

"Wherefore I abhor myself, and repent in dust and ashes." (Job 42:6)

Am I praying for God's cleansing work in my heart? Am I asking His forgiveness for my sin?

"Search me, O God, and know my heart: try me, and know my thoughts: and see if there be any wicked way in me, and lead me in the way everlasting." (Psalm 139:23-24)

"Wash me throughly from mine iniquity, and cleanse me from my sin." (Psalm 51:2)

"Create in me a clean heart, O God; and renew a right spirit within me." (Psalm 51:10)

Do I believe that God, because of Christ's work, will forgive me when I confess and repent of my sins?

"Come now, and let us reason together, saith the LORD: though your sins be as scarlet, they shall be as white as snow; though they be red like crimson, they shall be as wool. If ye be willing and obedient, ye shall eat the good of the land: but if ye refuse and rebel, ye shall be devoured with the sword: for the mouth of the LORD hath spoken it." (Isaiah 1:18-20)

"If we confess our sins, he is faithful and just to forgive us our sins, and to cleanse us from all unrighteousness." (1 John 1:9)

"I, even I, am he that blotteth out thy transgressions for mine own sake, and will not remember thy sins." (Isaiah 43:25)

"For thou, Lord, art good, and ready to forgive; and plenteous in mercy unto all them that call upon thee." (Psalm 86:5)

Am I confessing my sin to my parents or others I have offended?

"Confess your faults one to another, and pray one for another, that ye may be healed. The effectual fervent prayer of a righteous man availeth much." (James 5:16)

Am I ready to make restitution to those I have wronged? Am I righting the wrongs I have committed?

"Wash you, make you clean; put away the evil of your doings from before mine eyes; cease to do evil; learn to do well; seek judgment, relieve the oppressed, judge the fatherless, plead for the widow." (Isaiah 1:16-17)

"Bring forth therefore fruits meet for repentance." (Matthew 3:8)

"If a soul sin, and commit a trespass against the LORD, and lie unto his neighbour in that which was delivered him to keep, or in fellowship, or in a thing taken away by violence, or hath deceived his neighbour; or have found that which was lost, and lieth concerning it, and sweareth falsely; in any of all these that a man doeth, sinning therein: then it shall be, because he hath sinned, and is guilty, that he shall restore that which he took violently away, or the thing which he hath deceitfully gotten, or that which was delivered him to keep, or the lost thing which he found, or all that about which he hath sworn falsely; he shall even restore it in the principal, and shall add the fifth part more thereto, and give it unto him to whom it appertaineth, in the day of his trespass offering." (Leviticus 6:2-5)

Am I praying for God to give me the grace and strength to forsake my sinful attitudes and actions?

"And he said unto me, My grace is sufficient for thee: for my strength is made perfect in weakness. Most gladly therefore will I rather glory in my infirmities, that the power of Christ may rest upon me." (2 Corinthians 12:9)

"There hath no temptation taken you but such as is common to man: but God is faithful, who will not suffer you to be tempted above that ye are able; but will with the temptation also make a way to escape, that ye may be able to bear it." (1 Corinthians 10:13)

"Seeing then that we have a great high priest, that is passed into the heavens, Jesus the Son of God, let us hold fast our profession. For we have not an high priest which cannot be touched with the feeling of our infirmities; but was in all points tempted like as we are, yet without sin. Let us therefore come boldly unto the throne of grace, that we may obtain mercy, and find grace to help in time of need." (Hebrews 4:14-16)

Am I showing evidence of my repentance by departing from my sin and pursuing obedience?

"Depart from evil, and do good; seek peace, and pursue it." (Psalm 34:14)

"That ye put off concerning the former conversation the old man, which is corrupt according to the deceitful lusts; and be renewed in the spirit of your mind; and that ye put on the new man, which after God is created in righteousness and true holiness." (Ephesians 4:22-24)

"Now therefore, amend your ways and your doings, and obey the voice of the LORD your God; then the LORD will relent concerning the doom that He has pronounced against you." (Jeremiah 26:13, NKJV)

Am I committed to developing a loving, humble, and obedient relationship with God through Bible-reading, prayer, and fellowship with other believers?

"Wherefore lay apart all filthiness and superfluity of naughtiness, and receive with meekness the engrafted word, which is able to save your souls." (James 1:21)

"Wherewithal shall a young man cleanse his way? by taking heed thereto according to thy word. With my whole heart have I sought thee: O let me not wander from thy commandments." (Psalm 119:9-10)

"Watch and pray, that ye enter not into temptation: the spirit indeed is willing, but the flesh is weak." (Matthew 26:41)

"And let us consider one another to provoke unto love and to good works: not forsaking the assembling of ourselves together, as the manner of some is; but exhorting one another: and so much the more, as ye see the day approaching." (Hebrews 10:24-25)

Am I committed to memorizing Scripture as a means of renewing my mind and resisting temptation?

"Thy word have I hid in mine heart, that I might not sin against thee." (Psalm 119:11)

"I will delight myself in thy statutes: I will not forget thy word." (Psalm 119:16)

"And be not conformed to this world: but be ye transformed by the renewing of your mind, that ye may prove what is that good, and acceptable, and perfect, will of God." (Romans 12:2)

"For the word of God is quick, and powerful, and sharper than any twoedged sword, piercing even to the dividing asunder of soul and spirit, and of the joints and marrow, and is a discerner of the thoughts and intents of the heart." (Hebrews 4:12)

Am I humbly placing myself under the authority of my parents as God's delegated authorities in my life?

"Submit yourselves to every ordinance of man for the Lord's sake: whether it be to the king, as supreme; or unto governors, as unto them that are sent by him for the punishment of evildoers, and for the praise of them that do well. For so is the will of God, that with well doing ye may put to silence the ignorance of foolish men." (1 Peter 2:13-15)

"Let every soul be subject unto the higher powers. For there is no power but of God: the powers that be are ordained of God." (Romans 13:1)

"Children, obey your parents in all things: for this is well pleasing unto the Lord." (Colossians 3:20)

Projects for Further Study

Establish a habit of fervent prayer and dependence on God.

- Devote a special portion of each day to prayer. Live your life in total dependence on God, expressed through an attitude of constant prayer, speaking to God as you go through the day, seeking His wisdom and help when you encounter problems or temptations, praising Him for the constant manifestations of His love and control of all things.

- When submission comes with great difficulty and you are tempted to say more than you should to your parents, pour out your heart to God. Like King David, voice your discouragements, the injustices you experience, the frustrations you feel, and praise God for His unchanging faithfulness, His limitless power, His all-encompassing wisdom.

- Pray the words of Scripture back to God. Read the Psalms as prayers. Read the passages that describe godly parents, praying for God to do His changing work in your parents' hearts. Pray through the passages that outline the characteristics of the godly son or daughter, seeking God's grace to repent of wrong attitudes and actions.

- Keep a record of prayer requests and note each answer. Remember, the answer may not always be "yes," or the answer may come in a different form than you are expecting. For example, the answer to a request for a more understanding father may come in the form of God transforming you into a more understanding child!

Study the book of Proverbs.

The entire book of Proverbs is addressed to sons. Read the entire book, recording any advice that is given specifically to "my son" and any verses that give wisdom that pertains specifically to sons and daughters. Summarize your findings. How can you start applying the wisdom of these verses in your life? Outline a plan.

Study the examples of different sons and daughters in the Bible.

- Study daughters such as Miriam, Lot's daughters, Rebekah, Rachel, Leah, Ruth (as daughter-in-law), Dinah, Michal, and Esther (in her role under her cousin Mordecai's authority). Note Bible references that refer to each daughter and the events in her life. Read these passages carefully, and record what each woman did right or wrong and how her decisions and behavior affected her life and the lives of her parents and family.

- In the same manner, study sons such as Cain, Abel, Seth, Isaac, Jacob, Esau, Joseph and the rest of Jacob's sons, Moses, Samuel, Eli's sons, Samson, Jonathan, Absalom, Amnon, Solomon, and Adonijah.

- Apply these observations to your own life, and record specific areas in which, with God's help, you need to change. Rejoice, too, when you see the blessings that ultimately came to those sons and daughters who were faithful to God and their parents. God keeps His Word, both when we disobey and when we obey!

Study the lives of other godly young men in Scripture.

Study the lives of Daniel, Shadrach, Meshach, Abednego, and David. Scripture does not tell us much about the relationships of these young men with their parents, but we can learn from their examples of godly courage and obedience. Note the passages that tell about each person, and record your observations about their words, attitudes, and actions. What can you learn from each of these young men?

Study Jesus' example of submission to His Father.

Read the Gospels, noting each demonstration of Jesus' submission to God the Father. What things did Jesus do as the representative of His Father? In what situations did He submit His will to the will of His Father? What did He say was His purpose on earth?

What can you learn from His example that will help you better submit to your father and mother? Write down specific ideas and commit yourself to putting these ideas into action.

Study the parable of the prodigal son.

Read Luke 15:11-32. Note the words and actions of the son who left his father. Then note the words and actions of the elder son. What can you learn from this parable? Do you have the attitudes of either of these sons?

Study the following examples of repentance in Scripture. What does repentance involve? Did all these people truly repent?

- The Israelites – Judges 10:15-16
- David – 2 Samuel 11 and 12
- The Ninevites – Jonah 3:5-8
- Zacchaeus – Luke 19:1-8
- Josiah – 2 Kings 22:1-20
- Saul – 1 Samuel 15:1-30

Study Psalm 51.

What do you learn about repentance from this Psalm? List all that David asks of God? What does he confess? What does he say pleases God?

Study Deuteronomy 28.

The Bible very clearly delineates the blessings that come from obedience and the cursings that result from disobedience. We know that a believer, devoted to his Lord and to obeying His Word, will not live a life free of trials and hardship. God chooses to bring glory to Himself in ways we do not always understand. But Scripture also makes it clear that the general pattern for a life marked by obedience is one of great blessing.

Deuteronomy 28 is one of the passages of Scripture that lists in detail the ways in which God will bless and curse, depending on our response to God and His Word. Verse 2 reads, "And all these blessings shall come on thee, and overtake thee, if thou shalt hearken unto the voice of the LORD thy God."

Verse 15 tells us, "But it shall come to pass, if thou wilt not hearken unto the voice of the LORD thy God, to observe to do all his commandments and his statutes which I command thee this day; that all these curses shall come upon thee, and overtake thee."

- Study this listing of blessings and cursings. Note each **blessing**, listing them under various categories such as "How My Family Will Be Affected," "How My Labor Will Be Affected," etc.

- Note each **cursing**, again listing them under various categories, "How My Health Will Be Affected," "How My Thinking Will Be Affected," "How My Children Will Be Affected," "How My Labor Will Be Affected," etc.

- Review your findings and meditate on their meaning in your life. How is your family being affected by your attitude toward God and the authority He exercises over you through your parents? How is your health being affected by your willing submission or stubborn rebellion? How is your use of time affected? How productive is your life? Is God calling you to repentance?

Study the consequences of accepting and rejecting the counsel of others.

Using a concordance and a topical Bible, study verses dealing with reproof, counsel, rebuke, and instruction. Note each reference and the teaching of each passage. Summarize what you have found. What are the results of listening to good counsel and godly reproof? What happens to those who refuse to accept counsel?

Study what the Bible says about rebellious children.

Study passages in Scripture that describe the lives of obedient and disobedient (or rebellious) children. **Nave's Topical Bible** will be useful in this study. Read verses listed under the subheadings of "Good" and "Wicked" in the listing for "Children." What do you learn about "good children?" What do you learn about "wicked children?" What principles can you apply as you respond to the authority and leadership of your parents?

Write a letter to your parents.

List your parents' good traits and the specific ways they have blessed and served you. Then write a letter of gratitude to your parents. Be very specific as you thank them for their example and for the investment they have made in your life.

Examine your attitude toward other authorities that God has placed over you.

Study Question No. 124 and its answer in the **Westminster Larger Catechism** (see page VII). How are we to apply the Fifth Commandment to other superior-inferior relationships?

Reread this book, applying questions and Scripture to other relationships of authority in which God has placed you.

How are you doing under the authority of grandparents, teachers, employers, pastors, governmental authorities, and other elders and leaders under whom God has placed you?

Confess any sin in the relationships and commit to an attitude of reverence and submission.

Study examples of those in the Bible who chose to openly question their authority's right to rule over them.

Use a concordance to help you locate passages about the following people:

- Miriam
- Aaron
- Dathan and Abiram
- Absalom

Carefully read the accounts of their lives, paying special attention to the passages that describe their criticism of or resistance to their authorities. Note all your observations.

What did each person do that was wrong?

What were their apparent motivations?

What were the results in their lives and in the lives of those around them?

Study I Corinthians 13.

- List each positive quality of love, as described in this passage.
- List each action that this passage says love does not do.
- Study the passage in other translations.
- Rewrite verses 4 through 7, replacing the word "charity" with the word "I" or your own name.
- Pray for God to reveal areas in which you are not showing love to your parents.
- Using your list of the positive qualities of love, write very specific actions you can take to express each quality of godly love to your parents.
- Using your list of the things that love does not do, write very specific ways in which you have been unloving to your parents. Next to each of these ways write a positive action that you will take as you repent of these sins.
- Memorize the passage.

Study the meaning of the answers to Questions 127 and 128 of the Westminster Larger Catechism (see pages VII and VIII).

Use the definitions from **Noah Webster's 1828 American Dictionary of the English Language** listed on pages 115-122 to help you better understand the meaning of the words used in the catechism. Then write a paraphrase of the catechism answers, using what you have learned in your study of the words' definitions.

The honor which inferiors owe to their superiors is:

- All due reverence in heart, word, and behavior,

- Prayer and thanksgiving for them,

- Imitation of their virtues and graces,

- Willing obedience to their lawful commands and counsels,

- Due submission to their corrections,

- Fidelity to, defense and maintenance of their persons and authority,

- According to their several ranks, and the nature of their places,

- Bearing with their infirmities, and covering them in love,

- That so they may be an honor to them and to their government.

The sins of inferiors against their superiors are:

- All neglect of the duties required toward them;

- Envying at, contempt of, and rebellion against, their persons and places,

- In their lawful counsels, commands, and corrections;

- Cursing, mocking, and all such refractory and scandalous carriage,

- As proves a shame and dishonor to them and their government.

Definitions of the Words
Used in the Westminster Larger Catechism:

These definitions are taken from **Noah Webster's 1828 American Dictionary of the English Language.** *The Westminster Catechism was written in the 1600's, and the meanings of many English words have changed since that time. Noah Webster's definitions, compiled in the 1800's, offer us a clearer understanding of English as it was used when and soon after the catechism was written. (These definitions are excerpts from the complete definitions supplied by Webster. Refer to the complete dictionary for further study, if desired.)*

Authority:

1. Legal power, or a right to command or to act.

2. The power derived from opinion, respect or esteem.

Bear with:

To endure what is unpleasant, to be indulgent; to forbear to resent, oppose, or punish.

Behavior:

Manner of behaving, whether good or bad; conduct; manners; carriage of oneself, with respect to propriety, or morals; deportment. It expresses external appearance or action; sometimes in a particular character; more generally in the common duties of life; as, our future destiny depends on our **behavior** in this life.

Carriage:

In a moral sense, the manner of carrying one's self; behavior; conduct; deportment; personal manners.

Commands:

The right or power of governing with chief or exclusive authority. The mandate uttered; the order given.

Contempt:

1. The act of despising; the act of viewing or considering and treating as mean, vile and worthless; disdain; hatred of what is mean or deemed vile. This word is one of the strongest expressions of a mean opinion which the language affords.

2. In law, disobedience of the rules and orders of a court, which is a punishable offense.

   [**Contemptuous:** Haughty; insolent; scornful.]

Correction:

1. The act of bringing back, from error or deviation, to a just standard, as to truth, rectitude, justice, or propriety.

2. The counteraction of what is inconvenient or hurtful in its effects.

Counsels:

1. Advice; opinion, or instruction, given upon request or otherwise for directing the judgment or conduct of another; opinion given upon deliberation or consultation. ["Thou hast not hearkened to my **counsels**." 2 Chronicles 25]

2. Purpose; design; will; decree.

Cover:

1. To overspread the surface of a thing with another substance.

2. To hide or conceal by something overspread.

3. To conceal by some intervening object.

4. To clothe, as to **cover** with a robe or mantle.

5. To overwhelm.

6. To conceal from notice or punishment.

7. To wrap, enfold, envelop, as to **cover** a package of goods.

8. To shelter, to protect, to defend. A squadron of horse **covered** the troops on the retreat.

Cursing:

Execration; the uttering of a curse; a dooming to vexation or misery.

[**Curse:** Malediction; the expression of a wish of evil to another.]

[**To curse:** To utter a wish of evil against one; to call for mischief or injury to fall upon.]

Defense:

1. Any thing that opposes attack, violence, danger, or injury; any thing that secures the person, the rights or the possessions of men; fortification; guard; protection; security. A wall, a parapet, a ditch, or a garrison, is the **defense** of a city or fortress. ["The Almighty is the **defense** of the righteous." Psalm 59]

2. Vindication; justification; apology; that which repels or disproves a charge or accusation.

Dishonor:

To disgrace; to bring reproach or shame on; to stain the character of; to lessen reputation.

Due:

That which office, rank, station, social relations, or established rules of right or decorum, require to be given, paid or done.

Example: Respect and obedience to parents and magistrates are their **due**.

Duties:

1. That which a person owes to another; that which a person is bound, by any natural, moral, or legal obligation, to pay, do or perform. Obedience to princes, magistrates and laws is the **duty** of every citizen and subject; obedience, kindness, and respect to parents are **duties** of children; fidelity to friends is a **duty**; reverence, obedience, and prayer to God are indispensable **duties**; the government and religious instruction of children are **duties** of parents which they cannot neglect without guilt.

2. Forbearance of that which is forbid by morality, law, justice, or propriety. It is our **duty** to refrain from lewdness, intemperance, profaneness and injustice.

3. Obedience; submission.

4. Act of reverence or respect. ["They both did **duty** to their lady." Spenser]

Envying:

1. Mortification experienced at the supposed prosperity and happiness of another.

2. Ill will at others, on account of some supposed superiority.

Fidelity:

1. Faithfulness; careful and exact observance of duty, or performance of obligations. We expect **fidelity** in a public minister, in an agent or trustee, in a domestic servant, in a friend.

2. Firm adherence to a person or party with which one is united, or to which one is bound; loyalty; as the **fidelity** of subjects to their king or government; the **fidelity** of a tenant or liege to his lord.

3. Observance of the marriage covenant, as the **fidelity** of a husband or wife.

4. Honesty; veracity; adherence to the truth; as the **fidelity** of a witness.

Government:

1. Direction; regulation. These precepts will serve for the **government** of our conduct.

2. The exercise of authority; direction and restraint exercised over the actions of men in communities, societies or states.

3. The exercise of authority by a parent or householder. Children are often ruined by a neglect of **government** in parents.

4. An empire, kingdom or state; any territory over which the right of sovereignty is extended.

Graces:

1. Favor; good will; kindness; disposition to oblige another.

2. Virtuous or religious affection or disposition, as a liberal disposition, faith, meekness, humility, patience, etc., proceeding from divine influence.

3.   *Natural or acquired excellence. Any endowment that recommends the possessor to others.*

Heart:

1.   *The chief part; the vital part; the vigorous or efficacious part.*

2.   *The seat of the affections and passions, as of love, joy, grief, enmity, courage, pleasure, etc. "The **heart** is deceitful above all things . . ." (Jeremiah 17:9a)*

3.   *By a metonymy, **heart** is used for an affection or passion, particularly for love. " . . . The king's **heart** was toward Absalom." (2 Samuel 14:1b)*

4.   *The seat of understanding; as an understanding **heart**.*

5.   *The seat of the will; hence, secret purposes, intentions or designs. "There are many devices in a man's **heart** . . ." (Proverbs 19:21a)*

6.   *Sometimes **heart** is used for the will, or determined purpose. "The **heart** of the sons of men is fully set in them to do evil." (Ecclesiastes 8:11b)*

7.   *Secret thoughts; recesses of the mind [Michal "saw king David leaping and dancing before the Lord, and she despised him in her **heart**." 2 Samuel 6:16b]*

8.   *Secret meaning; real intention.*

9.   *Conscience, or sense of good or ill. "Every man's **heart** and conscience -- doth either like or disallow it." (Hooker)*

Honor:

1.   *The esteem due or paid to worth; high estimation. ["A prophet is not without **honor**, except in his own country." Matthew 13:57]*

2.   *That which honors; he or that which confers dignity; as, the chancellor is an **honor** to his profession.*

3.   *That which adorns; ornament; decoration.*

Imitation:

The act of following in manner, or of copying in form; the act of attempting a similitude of any thing, or of attempting a resemblance.

Inferior:

A person who is younger, or of a lower station or rank in society.

Infirmity:

1.   *An unsound or unhealthy state of the body; weakness; feebleness. Old age is subject to **infirmities**.*

2.   *Weakness of mind; fault; failing; foible. ["A friend should bear a friend's **infirmities**." Shakespeare]*

3.   *Weakness of resolution.*

4.   *Defect; imperfection; weakness; as the **infirmities** of a constitution of government.*

Lawful:

1. Agreeable to law; conformable to law; allowed by law; legal; legitimate. That is deemed **lawful** which no law forbids, but many things are **lawful** which are not expedient.

2. Constituted by law; rightful; as the **lawful** owner of lands.

Love:

1. An affection of the mind excited by beauty and worth of any kind, or by the qualities of an object which communicate pleasure, sensual or intellectual. It is opposed to hatred. The **love** of God is the first duty of man, and this springs from just views of his attributes or excellencies of character, which afford the highest delight to the sanctified heart. Esteem and reverence constitute ingredients in this affection, and a fear of offending him is its inseparable effect.

2. Benevolence; good will. ["God is **love**." 1 John 4:16b]

Maintenance:

1. Sustenance; support by means of supplies of food, clothing, and other conveniences.

2. Support; protection; defense; vindication; as the **maintenance** of right or just claims.

Mocking:

Imitating in contempt; mimicking; ridiculing by mimicry; treating with sneers and scorn; defeating; deluding.

[**To mock:** To deride; to laugh at; to ridicule; to treat with scorn or contempt.]

Neglect:

1. Omission; forbearance to do anything that can be done or that requires to be done. **Neglect** may be from carelessness or intention. The **neglect** of business is the cause of many failures, but **neglect** of economy is more frequent and more injurious.

2. Negligence; habitual want of regard.

Obedience:

1. Proper submission to authority. That which duty requires implies dignity of conduct rather than servility. Voluntary **obedience** alone can be acceptable to God.

2. The performance of what is required or enjoined by authority, or the abstaining from what is prohibited, in compliance with command or prohibition.

Person:

1. Character of office.

2. An individual human being consisting of body and soul. We apply the word to living beings only, possessed of a rational nature.

Place:

1. Office; employment; official station. The man has a **place** under the government. ["Do you your office, or give up your **place**." Shakespeare]

2. Station in life; calling; occupation; condition. All, in their several **places**, perform their duty.

Prayer:

A solemn address to the Supreme Being, consisting of **adoration**, or an expression of our sense of God's glorious perfections, **confession** of our sins, **supplication** for mercy and forgiveness, **intercession** for blessings on others, and **thanksgiving**, or an expression of gratitude to God for his mercies and benefits.

Rank:

1. Degree of elevation in civil life or station; the order of elevation or of subordination. We say, all **ranks** and orders of men; every man's dress and behavior should correspond with his **rank**; the highest and the lowest **ranks** of men or other intelligent beings.

2. Class; order; division; any portion or number of things to which place, degree or order is assigned.

Rebellion:

1. An open and avowed renunciation of the authority of the government to which one owes allegiance; or the taking of arms traitorously to resist the authority of lawful government; revolt.

2. Open resistance to lawful authority.

Refractory:

1. A person obstinate in opposition or disobedience. Obstinate opposition.

2. Sullen or perverse in opposition or disobedience; obstinate in non-compliance. Obstinately unyielding.

Required:

Demanded; needed; necessary.

Reverence:

Fear mingled with respect and esteem. Veneration.
[Example: "When quarrels and factions are carried openly, it is a sign that **reverence** of government is lost." Bacon]

Scandalous:

1. Giving offense.

2. Disgraceful to reputation; that brings shame or infamy.

    [**Scandal:** Defamatory speech or report; something uttered which is false and injurious to reputation.]

Shame:

1. A painful sensation excited by a consciousness of guilt, or of having done something which injures reputation; or by the exposure of that which nature or modesty prompts us to conceal.

2. The cause or reason of shame; that which brings reproach, and degrades a person in the estimation of others.

3. Reproach; ignominy; derision; contempt. ["Ye have borne the **shame** of the heathen." Ezekiel 36:6]

Submission:

1. The act of yielding to power or authority; surrender of the person and power to the control or government of another.

2. Acknowledgment of inferiority or dependence; humble or suppliant behavior.

3. Yielding of one's will to the will or appointment of a superior without murmuring.

Superior:

1. One who is more advanced in age. Old persons or elders are the **superiors** of the young.

2. One who is more elevated in rank or office.

Thanksgiving:

The act of rendering thanks or expressing gratitude for favors or mercies.

[**Thankful:** Grateful; impressed with a sense of kindness received, and ready to acknowledge it. We should celebrate the Lord's Supper with a **thankful** remembrance of his suffering and death.]

Virtues:

1. Strength; that substance or quality of physical bodies, by which they act and produce effects on other bodies. In this literal and proper sense, we speak of the **virtue** or **virtues** of plants in medicine, and the **virtues** of drugs. In decoctions, the **virtues** of plants are extracted.

2. Bravery; valor. This was the predominant signification of "virtus" among the Romans.

3. Moral goodness; the practice of moral duties and the abstaining from vice, or a conformity of life and conversation to the moral law.

4. A particular moral excellence; as the **virtue** of temperance, of chastity, of charity.

Willing:

1. Free to do or grant; having the mind inclined; disposed; not adverse. Let every man give who is able and **willing**.

2. Pleased; desirous. ["Felix, **willing** to show the Jews a pleasure." Acts 24:7b]

3. Ready; prompt. ["He stoop'd with weary wings and **willing** feet." Milton]

4. Chosen; received of choice or without reluctance; as, to be held in **willing** chains.

5. Spontaneous. ["No spouts of blood run **willing** from a tree." Dryden]

Word:

1. An articulate or vocal sound, or a combination of articulate and vocal sounds, uttered by the human voice, and by custom expressing an idea or ideas; a single component part of human speech or language.

2. Talk; discourse.

3. Language; living speech; oral expression. The message was delivered by **word** of mouth.

4. Promise. He gave me his **word** he would pay me.

Additional Resources

Parents, if you are looking for further guidance as you train your children, we recommend the following practical books and charts:

Age of Opportunity: A Biblical Guide to Parenting Teens, by Paul David Tripp

An excellent Bible-based guide for parents of teenagers, this very practical book shows parents how to seize the countless opportunities to deepen communication, instruct, and learn from their teenagers.

The Blessing Chart

*This chart is designed to help you acknowledge and reward godly attitudes and behavior, in a way that is patterned after Scripture. Based on the ideas listed in **For Instruction in Righteousness**, this chart comes with a booklet of ideas for rewards that relate to God's rewards in our lives. The left-hand column lists good character qualities, with cartoon drawings. The center column quotes Scripture verses that tell how God blesses us when these qualities are present in our lives. The third column is blank, for you to write in the agreed-upon rewards for positive behavior. This chart offers a good balance for moms who specialize in seeing what the kids are doing wrong! We found that our more strong-willed children really responded to encouragement when we noticed them doing what was right! Available from Doorposts.*

A Checklist for Parents, by Pam Forster

*A series of 25 questions designed to **help parents examine themselves in light of God's Word**. Organized under 6 areas of responsibility (love, prayer, instruction, protection, provision, and example), each question is followed by Scripture verses which explain what God requires of us as parents. Use as a tool for prayer times, Scripture memorization, and for preparing your children for parenthood.*

Family Circles, by Pam Forster

A kit of materials to help you assemble a life-changing visual aid for your family. Build relationships with your children as you spend individual time with each child during the day -- for special projects, prayer, Bible study, bed-time snuggling, etc.

For Instruction in Righteousness, by Pam Forster

A topical guide for parents, listing Scripture on over 50 common areas of sin. Each chapter gives Bible verses that tell about the sin, what the Bible says will happen to a person who indulges in that sin, parallel ideas for discipline, simple, instructive object lessons based on Scriptural teaching about the sin, verses that explain how God blesses those who resist the sin, parallel ideas for rewards and encouragement, fully quoted memory verses, Bible stories that illustrate obedience and disobedience. Spiral or 3-ring binding. Available from Doorposts.

The Heart of Anger, by Lou Priolo

An excellent book that offers guidance to parents of angry children. Helps parents examine their own shortcomings, and gives practical, biblical help for curing the problem of anger.

The If-Then Chart

This is a chart designed to help you be more consistent in disciplining your children. The chart is divided into 3 columns. The left-hand column lists common areas of misbehavior (arguing, complaining, etc.), each illustrated with a simple cartoon. The center column gives a Scripture verse related to each sin. The third column is blank, for you to write in the agreed-upon consequences for each misbehavior. The instruction sheet offers suggestions for discipline. This chart has made discipline much easier in our home! Available from Doorposts.

Plants Grown Up, by Pam Forster

A notebook full of goals and projects especially designed for sons on their way to manhood. Choose from hundreds of activities and Bible study ideas to help your sons prepare for their future roles as employees, employers, husbands, fathers, church and community leaders. Designed to use throughout the years as your son matures, activities are appropriate for a very young boy and on until he is ready to launch into career, marriage, and raising your grandchildren! 535 pages, spiral-bound. Available from Doorposts.

Polished Cornerstones, by Pam Forster

Like **Plants Grown Up**, but for girls! Choose from 600 pages of activities and Bible study ideas to help your daughters prepare for their future roles as friends, homemakers, wives, mothers, church and community members. One copy works for all daughters of all ages! Spiral-bound. Available from Doorposts.

Standing on the Promises, by Douglas Wilson

A thorough handbook of biblical childrearing, this book addresses the covenantal nature of the family, God's promises to parents, and the duties God has assigned to parents. Solid foundational material for all fathers and mothers.

Teach Them Diligently, by Lou Priolo

A powerful and easy-to-understand approach to using Scripture in child training. Our personal favorite.